# Reading & Writing
# Pyramids of Giza

Australia • Brazil • Mexico • Singapore • United Kingdom • United States

National Geographic Learning,
a Cengage Company

**Reading & Writing, Pyramids of Giza**

**Lauri Blass, Mari Vargo, Keith S. Folse,
April Muchmore-Vokoun, Elena Vestri**

Publisher: Sherrise Roehr

Executive Editor: Laura LeDréan

Managing Editor: Jennifer Monaghan

Digital Implementation Manager,
Irene Boixareu

Senior Media Researcher: Leila Hishmeh

Director of Global Marketing: Ian Martin

Regional Sales and National Account
Manager: Andrew O'Shea

Content Project Manager: Ruth Moore

Senior Designer: Lisa Trager

Manufacturing Planner: Mary Beth
Hennebury

Composition: Lumina Datamatics

© 2020 Cengage Learning, Inc.

ALL RIGHTS RESERVED. No part of this work covered by the copyright herein
may be reproduced or distributed in any form or by any means, except as
permitted by U.S. copyright law, without the prior written permission of the
copyright owner.

"National Geographic", "National Geographic Society" and the Yellow Border
Design are registered trademarks of the National Geographic Society
® Marcas Registradas

For permission to use material from this text or product,
submit all requests online at **cengage.com/permissions**
Further permissions questions can be emailed to
**permissionrequest@cengage.com**

Student Edition: Reading & Writing, Pyramids of Giza
ISBN-13: 978-0-357-13833-5

**National Geographic Learning**
20 Channel Center Street
Boston, MA 02210
USA

Locate your local office at **international.cengage.com/region**

Visit National Geographic Learning online at **ELTNGL.com**
Visit our corporate website at **www.cengage.com**

Printed in Hong Kong
Print Number: 04   Print Year: 2023

# PHOTO CREDITS

**1** © Monica Serrano, NGM Staff; Tony Schick Source**:** Steven E. Platnick and Claire L. Parkinson, NASA Goddard Space Flight, **2-3** Ignacio Ayestaran/National Geographic Creative, **5** Albert Gea/Reuters, **11** (t) © Jer Thorp, (br) Smith Collection/Gado/Getty Images, **14** Robert Alexander/Getty **15** (tr) Lonely Planet Images/Getty Images, **16** Lam Yik Fei/Bloomberg via Getty Images, **24-25** © JOEL SARTORE/National Geographic Images, **26** © archana bhartia/Shutterstock.com, **27** © Jochen Tack/Alamy, **30** © J. Clarke/Taxi/Getty Images, **32** © OJO Images Ltd/Alamy, **34** ©lculig/iStockphoto.com, **36** © Rob Wilson/Shutterstock.com, **49** Gunter Marx/Alamy Stock Photo, **53** Sandy Huffaker/Getty Images, **55** © United Nations Photo Library, **59** Chris Rainier/Enduring Voices Project/National Geographic Creative, **62** Lynn Johnson/National Geographic Creative, **64** Lynn Johnson/National Geographic Creative, **73** Alex Hyde/NPL, **74** (bl) Tim McDonagh/National Geographic Creative, (br) Tim McDonagh/National Geographic Creative, **75** (t) Ryan Morris/National Geographic Creative, (br) Tim McDonagh/National Geographic Creative, **77** AF archive/Alamy Stock Photo, **78** National Geographic Creative, **80** Ryan Morris/National Geographic Creative, **81** © Yudhijit Bhattacharjee, **85** National Geographic Creative

# Scope and Sequence

# INFORMATION DESIGN 1

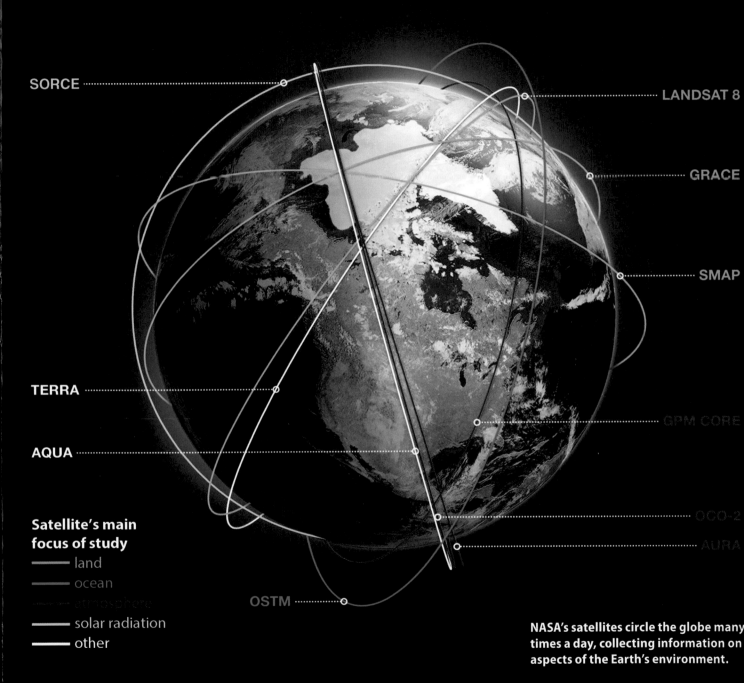

SORCE

LANDSAT 8

GRACE

SMAP

TERRA

GPM CORE

AQUA

OCO-2

AURA

**Satellite's main focus of study**
—— land
—— ocean
----- atmosphere
—— solar radiation
—— other

OSTM

**NASA's satellites circle the globe many times a day, collecting information on aspects of the Earth's environment.**

## ACADEMIC SKILLS

READING  Identifying arguments and counterarguments
WRITING  Writing a persuasive essay
GRAMMAR  Describing visual information
CRITICAL THINKING  Evaluating visual data

## THINK AND DISCUSS

1  What does the infographic above show?
2  What are some other ways in which information and data can be presented visually?

**A Look at the information on these pages and answer the questions.**

1. What does the infographic show?

2. Do you think it's an effective infographic? Why or why not?

**B Match the words and phrases in blue to their definitions.**

_____ (v) to communicate

_____ (v) to be noticeable or easy to see

_____ (v) to understand the meaning of something

**Grille**
Made in: Germany
Company Headquarters: Germany

**Hood**
Made in: Netherlands
Company
Headquarters: Austria

**Gasoline engine**
Made in: Brazil
Company Headquarters: Brazil

**Diesel engine
(not shown)**
Made in: Japan
Company Headquarters: Japan

**Front
and rear
bumpers**
Made in: U.K.
Company
Headquarters:
Canada

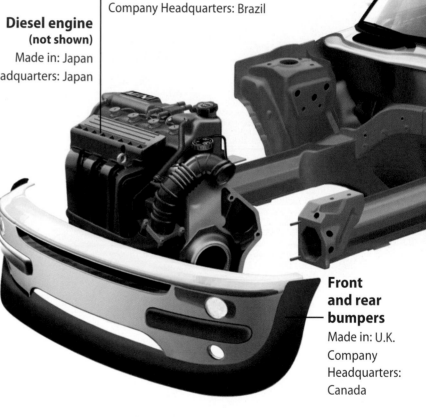

# UNDER THE HOOD

When you think of infographics, you might think of pie charts and line graphs—or you might picture more complex images such as the globe on the previous page. But infographics can take almost any form. With a single infographic, designers are now able to **convey** complicated information and help us **interpret** the meaning of vast data sets.

The infographic on these pages, for example, has a 3-D design that allows a viewer to understand a large amount of information about a car in a small amount of space. In the image, the outer shell of a BMW Mini has been lifted away from the car's body so that the viewer can see its inner workings. This treatment lets each piece of the car **stand out** as an individual part. In addition, the infographic allows a viewer to see a bigger story— although the car is made by a German company, it is actually a global product.

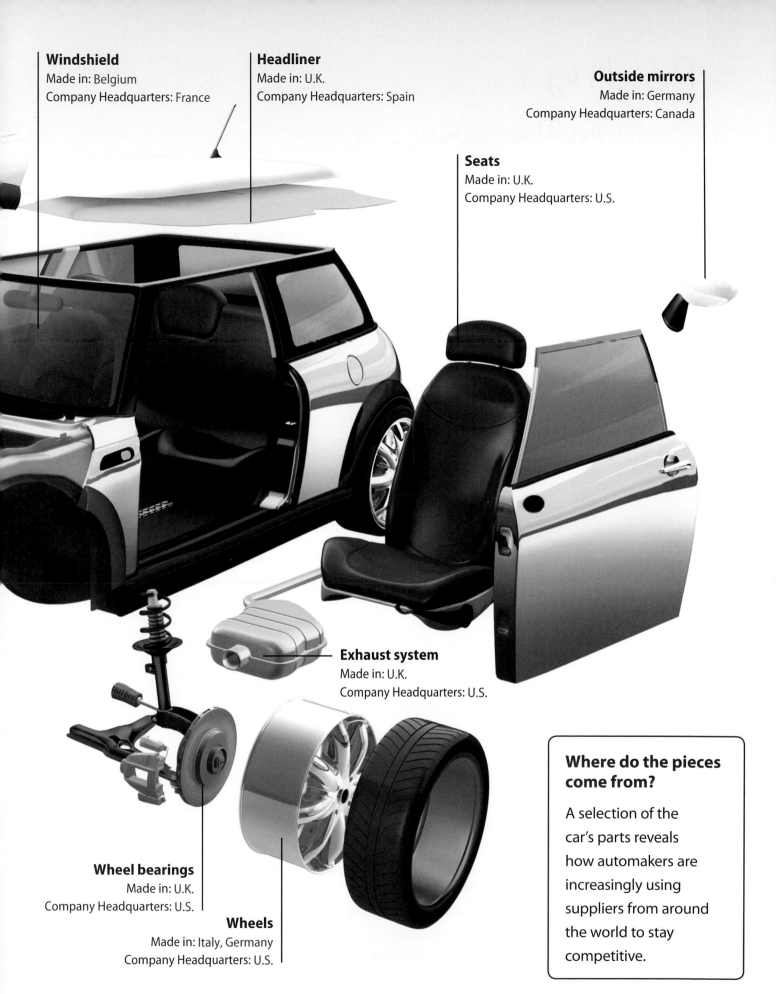

**Windshield**
Made in: Belgium
Company Headquarters: France

**Headliner**
Made in: U.K.
Company Headquarters: Spain

**Outside mirrors**
Made in: Germany
Company Headquarters: Canada

**Seats**
Made in: U.K.
Company Headquarters: U.S.

**Exhaust system**
Made in: U.K.
Company Headquarters: U.S.

**Wheel bearings**
Made in: U.K.
Company Headquarters: U.S.

**Wheels**
Made in: Italy, Germany
Company Headquarters: U.S.

### Where do the pieces come from?

A selection of the car's parts reveals how automakers are increasingly using suppliers from around the world to stay competitive.

# Reading 1

## PREPARING TO READ

BUILDING VOCABULARY

**A** The words in **blue** below are used in Reading 1. Read the sentences. Then match the correct form of each word to its definition.

> Good journalists aim to present the news in an **objective** manner without inserting their own opinions into their reports.
>
> People with poor **vision** correct their eyesight by wearing glasses or contact lenses.
>
> In order to make their products seem more effective, companies might **deliberately** include **misleading** information in their advertisements.
>
> One **downside** to using information from the Internet is that the source may not be reliable.
>
> Most people have strong opinions about whale hunting. Not many people are **neutral** about the issue.
>
> When writing a report, it's important to check that the points make sense and don't contain **faulty** logic.

1. _____ (n) a disadvantage

2. _____ (adv) on purpose or intentionally

3. _____ (n) the ability to see

4. _____ (adj) containing mistakes; inaccurate

5. _____ (adj) based on facts, not personal bias

6. _____ (adj) not having an opinion about something

7. _____ (adj) making someone believe something that is not true

USING VOCABULARY

**B** Discuss these questions with a partner.

1. What do you think are the **downsides** to using information from the Internet?

2. What kinds of **misleading** information have you seen online?

BRAINSTORMING

**C** What are some benefits of infographics for people working in business, education, or journalism? Discuss with a partner.

PREDICTING

**D** Skim the first sentence of each paragraph in the reading passage. What do you think the passage is about? Check your idea as you read.

a. the purposes of different types of infographics

b. the history of data visualization

c. the pros and cons of using infographics

# THE RISE OF VISUAL DATA

Facebook CEO Mark Zuckerberg presents a graphic showing the global connections of Facebook users.

🎧 Track 1

A     Visual data—charts, maps, and infographics—are more prevalent[1] than ever. Every day, we are exposed to visual data in print, in online media, and in the apps we use. Why is visual data so common today? And are there any **downsides** to living in a world of visual data?

## THE POWER OF VISUALS

B     The human brain can **interpret** a complex concept more quickly when it is presented visually than when it is explained on printed text. A 2014 study at the Massachusetts Institute of Technology (MIT), for example, showed that humans can interpret an image of a "smiling couple" after seeing it for only 13 milliseconds—nearly 10 times faster than the blink of an eye. To explain all the details of the "smiling couple" in writing would take significantly longer. As Mary Potter, professor of brain and cognitive sciences at MIT, explains, "What **vision** does is find concepts. That's what the brain is doing all day long—trying to understand what we're looking at."

[1]Something that is **prevalent** is widespread or common.

Data visualization journalist and educator Alberto Cairo thinks that "words alone are not powerful enough to communicate effectively ... you also need visuals." Visual data is most effective when there is an "aha" moment—when the information provides "spontaneous insight." These visuals immediately create understanding of complex concepts. Cairo cites a chart (Figure 1) that shows the sudden rise in global temperatures as an example of this. With its sharp curve upward, the chart quickly **conveys** how rapidly our planet is warming.

Visual data also appears to make information seem more credible. A study carried out at Cornell University in New York showed that 67 percent of participants believed information when they read it in a document without a graph. However, when a graph was included, 96 percent believed the same information. Alberto Cairo agrees that "a message looks more scientific when you put charts in it." He points out that visual data can also mislead, because it makes textual information look more serious and academic than it perhaps is.

## THE PITFALLS OF VISUAL DATA

Even though graphs may look credible, they can be misleading, especially if **faulty** logic is used to present information. Figure 2, for example, shows the rise and fall of the performance of athletes who appeared on the cover of *Sports Illustrated* magazine. The graph appears to imply there is a cause-effect relationship between two events: being on the cover of the magazine leads to poor performance afterward.

In fact, athletes usually appear on magazine covers when they are at the peak of their performance. After this stage, it is most probable that athletes' performance will eventually decline. So, although there may be a correlation between two events, that does not mean that one event has a direct effect on the other.

Another way charts can mislead is when a scale is inappropriate. Figure 3 illustrates the effectiveness of two drugs, and there seems to be a big difference between them. However, the difference looks greater than it really is.

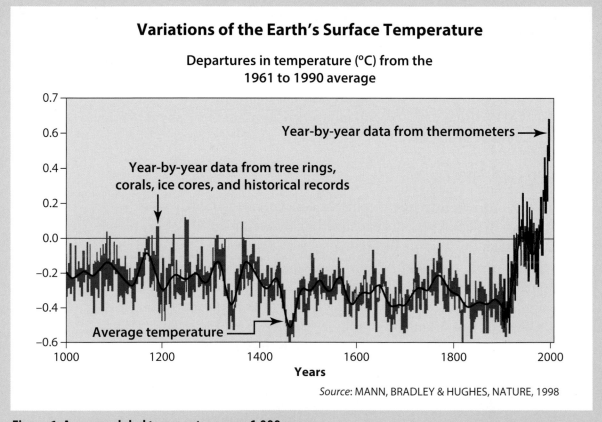

Figure 1: Average global temperature over 1,000 years

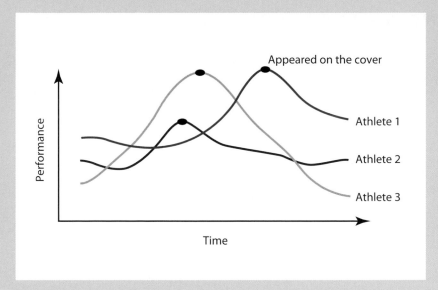

**Figure 2: Performance of athletes before and after appearing on the cover of *Sports Illustrated* magazine**

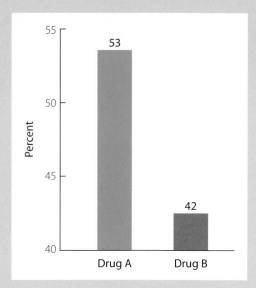

**Figure 3: Effectiveness of Drug A**

This is because the numbers on the vertical axis go only from 40 percent to 55 percent—making it look like Drug A is five times more effective than Drug B. In fact, the difference between the two drugs is only about 10 percent. In addition, the color of the bar for Drug A makes that data **stand out** more and seem more important—and positive—than Drug B.

Some visuals may be unintentionally misleading. Others, however, may be **deliberately** designed to influence the viewer. According to Cairo, deliberately **misleading** visuals are designed to make a point, not to objectively present facts. While he thinks this may be valid in advertising or PR, it's not a good example of **objective** journalistic communication. Cairo believes that while designers may never be able to approach information in a completely **neutral** way, they should at least try: "That is what journalism is."

## VISUALIZING THE FUTURE

According to Geoff McGhee—a data visualizer at Stanford University—new forms of visual data are pushing the boundaries of what we can process. Unlike traditional visual data, these new types of visuals use thousands of data points, such as the map showing global connections on Facebook (the first image in this reading passage). Many of these modern visualizations feature a huge number of thin, overlapping,[2] and semi-transparent[3] lines. The 3-D effect allows viewers to "see through" points to look at others behind.

Some journalists worry that complex visualizations such as these may make beautiful data art, but risk confusing readers instead of enlightening them. For Alberto Cairo, the key issue with visualization is not complexity or beauty, but whether the public is reliably informed. When creators of visual data are balanced and honest, he says, "great visualizations change people's mind for the better."

[2]When two lines are **overlapping**, part of one line covers part of the other line.
[3]If something is **semi-transparent**, you can see through it, but not completely.

# UNDERSTANDING THE READING

SUMMARIZING **A** Read the first sentence of a summary of the passage. Check (✓) three other sentences to complete the summary.

*Infographics are more common today, but data visualizers should take into consideration certain issues.*

☐ 1. Visual data is not as effective as text, but it is more interesting to look at and makes information seem more trustworthy.

☐ 2. It is easier and faster to interpret large amounts of information through visual data than through text.

☐ 3. There are many benefits to using visual data, but charts and graphs can be misleading.

☐ 4. Most infographics on the Internet unintentionally use incorrect data.

☐ 5. In the future, infographics will be easier to create and less confusing than they are now.

☐ 6. Data visualization may become more complex in the future, but it is important that it remains clear and accurate.

UNDERSTANDING DETAILS **B** Write answers to these questions. Then share your answers with a partner.

1. According to Alberto Cairo, when is visual data most effective?

   _____

2. What does Cairo think is one benefit of including charts in a document?

   _____

3. What ways of presenting visual data can result in inaccurate information? List three ways.

   _____

   _____

   _____

4. What is a main difference between modern infographics and traditional charts such as line graphs?

   _____

INTERPRETING VISUAL INFORMATION **C** Read the descriptions below. Match each one to a figure from the passage (1–3).

_____ a. the y-axis has a misleading scale

_____ b. shows a trend that is increasing

_____ c. presents a misleading comparison

_____ d. illustrates performance levels over time

_____ e. shows the relative success of two products

_____ f. provides quick insight into complex information

_____ g. implies an incorrect cause-effect relationship

_____ h. allows various data to be compared against an average

**D** Find and underline the following words in **bold** in the reading passage. Use context to identify their meanings. Match the sentence parts to complete the definitions.

1. Paragraph D: If something is **credible**, _____
2. Paragraph E: If you **imply** something, _____
3. Paragraph F: If there is a **correlation** between two things, _____
4. Paragraph H: If something is done **unintentionally**, _____

a. it is not done on purpose.
b. it is believable or trustworthy.
c. you suggest it without stating it directly.
d. there is a meaningful connection between them.

> **CRITICAL THINKING**   In order to **evaluate visual data**, ask yourself: Does the infographic show an accurate representation of relationships between two or more things, or is it biased to show one perspective? Is the scale misleading or exaggerated in some way? Is the creator of the infographic neutral?

**E** Study the two graphs below. How are they different?

_____

Which scale would be more suitable for each situation below?

_____ a. for looking in detail at the monthly changes in the U.S.'s GDP
_____ b. for comparing with another country's GDP in the same time period

**Falling Gross Domestic Product (GDP) in the United States**

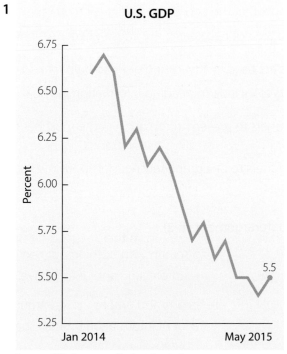

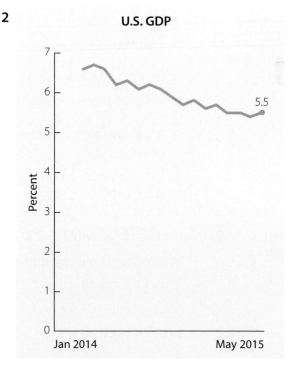

Source: U.S. Bureau of Labor Statistics

**F** Look back and find an infographic that you think best follows the principles of objective design. Find another infographic that you think could be improved. Discuss your reasons with a partner.

# DEVELOPING READING SKILLS

> ### READING SKILL Identifying Arguments and Counterarguments
>
> Writers often acknowledge counterarguments—the arguments on the other side of the issue—in addition to presenting their own arguments. Concession words and phrases are often used to signal counterarguments. Some examples are *while, even though, though,* and *although.*
>
>                                COUNTERARGUMENT                                     WRITER'S ARGUMENT
>
> ***While*** *it may seem difficult to make good infographics, <u>anyone can create them with the right software</u>.*

IDENTIFYING
ARGUMENTS

**A** Find the following concession words and phrases in the reading passage. Then underline the writer's argument and draw two lines under the counterargument.

1. even though (paragraph E)

2. although (paragraph F)

3. while (paragraph H)

4. while (paragraph H)

IDENTIFYING
ARGUMENTS

**B** Choose the correct paraphrase of each main argument in exercise A. Then share your answers with a partner.

1. a. Graphs that look impressive sometimes contain inaccurate information.

   b. Misleading information is sometimes included to make charts attractive.

2. a. More evidence is needed to show that the two events affect each other.

   b. Two events that are connected are not necessarily in a cause-effect relationship.

3. a. Deliberately misleading visuals are used in advertising or PR to help make a point.

   b. It is unacceptable for journalists to include misleading information in visual data.

4. a. It is important for graphic designers to present information in the most neutral way possible.

   b. It is impossible for graphic designers to be completely neutral about the issues they write about.

IDENTIFYING
COUNTERARGUMENTS

**C** Match each argument (a–c) to a counterargument (1–3).

1. While including charts and graphs is useful in reports, _____

2. Although charts and graphs may not always be necessary, _____

3. Though they sometimes seem simple, _____

a. a screen with nothing but text on it is uninteresting and unattractive.

b. charts and graphs can communicate a lot of information in small spaces.

c. they should be used only if they relate to the points made.

# Video

Jer Thorp created this graphic to show exoplanets—planets outside of our solar system—discovered by the Kepler space telescope.

326.01

# PAINTING WITH NUMBERS

## BEFORE VIEWING

**A** Read the caption above and discuss the answers to these questions with a partner.

PREDICTING

1. What might the different sizes and colors of the circles represent?
2. What do you think the locations of the circles represent?

**B** Read the information about data artists. In what ways are Thorp's and Nightingale's infographics similar? Discuss your answer with a partner.

LEARNING ABOUT THE TOPIC

Jer Thorp is a data artist—someone who combines art and science to better communicate complex information. According to Thorp, an early example of an infographic was by Florence Nightingale—a nurse during the Crimean War (1853–1856). One of her graphics (right) showed that, contrary to popular belief, most soldiers were dying of treatable diseases rather than from injuries during the war. Her work reduced soldiers' deaths by over 60 percent, and is an example of how infographics can change public opinion.

**Causes of death**

- disease
- injury
- other

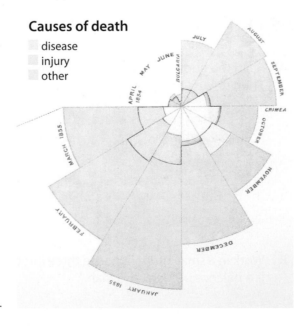

**C** The words in **bold** below are used in the video. Read the sentences. Then match the correct form of each word to its definition.

> Police use maps to **plot** the **incidence** of crimes in an area. This can help them identify areas that need extra security.
>
> A complicated issue can be explored from different **angles**.
>
> One **strategy** to creating an effective infographic is to use objective data.

1. _____ (n) the number of times an event happens

2. _____ (v) to mark data on a map or chart

3. _____ (n) a particular perspective of something

4. _____ (n) a way of doing something to achieve a goal

# WHILE VIEWING

**A** ▶ Watch the video. What benefits of using visual data are mentioned?

☐ 1. It makes data easier to remember.

☐ 2. It simplifies complex data.

☐ 3. It helps us see things we've never seen before.

☐ 4. It makes data more interesting.

**B** ▶ Watch the video again. Complete the sentences about what each graphic shows.

1. John Snow's map shows where people _____

   _____

2. The "Just Landed" visualization shows _____

   _____

# AFTER VIEWING

**A** Read the quote from the video about Thorp's "ooh-aah" approach to creating graphics. Then discuss the questions with a partner.

"The first thing I want people to do is I want them to say 'ooh' when they see the visualization, but that 'ooh' is useless unless there's an 'aah.' I want that learned moment that comes from really being able to discover something that you didn't understand before."

1. What makes people say "ooh" about an infographic?

2. What makes people say "aah"?

**B** Work in a small group. Choose three infographics in this book. For each, decide if there is a balance of "ooh" and "aah."

# Reading 2

## PREPARING TO READ

**A** The words and phrases in **blue** below are used in Reading 2. Complete the sentences with the correct form of the words or phrases. Use a dictionary to help you.

BUILDING VOCABULARY

| context | propose | publication | have to do with | reliance |
|---------|---------|-------------|-----------------|----------|
| universal | nevertheless | statistic | emphasize | gesture |

1. _____ such as comics and magazines tend to have more images, compared to journal articles that usually contain more data and _____ .

2. Sometimes, speakers use simple _____ while giving a speech, especially when they want to _____ certain points and draw people's attention to them.

3. People who create infographics may not be totally neutral about the data they are using. _____, Alberto Cairo thinks that they should try to present the data in the most objective way possible.

4. Although it is helpful to include visuals in an essay, you should make sure that they are suitable for the _____ in which they are used.

5. When you see a chart or graph, ask yourself: what does it _____ the topic?

6. Visuals such as photos and infographics are like a(n) _____ language—there is little _____ on text to convey meaning.

7. Data artist Jer Thorp _____ that we can use the "ooh-aah" approach when evaluating the effectiveness of visual information.

**B** Discuss these questions with a partner.

USING VOCABULARY

1. What are some common **gestures** in your culture or country? What do they mean?

2. What are some topics that have **universal** appeal around the world?

**C** Work with a partner. What does the color red make you think of? What about the color green?

BRAINSTORMING

**D** Look at the images and read the first paragraph of the reading passage. What kinds of cultural differences in visual design do you think you will read about? Discuss with a partner. Then check your ideas as you read.

PREDICTING

The colors and other visual cues in signs are often influenced by cultural preferences.

# VISUAL CULTURE

🎧 Track 2

When we think of language, we usually think of words, but visuals are also a part of communication. And like written language, visual symbols are not **universal**. An English speaker, for example, may place their hand near their chest as a **gesture** to mean "me," while a Japanese speaker is likely to point at their nose to indicate the same. Similarly, the way visual information is used can vary depending on the cultural **context**.

Take the color of money. Charles Apple, an American visual journalist, was working for a newspaper in South Africa when green was **proposed** as a color for the business section. The newspaper preferred blue, however, and for a simple reason: not every country has green money.

And that's not all. "In the United States, red usually has a connotation[1] of losses or deficits," Apple says, "but that's not true in all countries." Xan Sabaris, a Spanish infographic artist who has worked for the Beijing-based *China Daily*, agrees: "For the Western culture, red has negative connotations. In China, it's the opposite. You could see Chinese newspapers where stock market charts use green for negative values and red for positive ones."

Shapes are influenced by culture, too. Antonio Farach, from Honduras, and Adonis Durado, from the Philippines, both work at the *Times of Oman*. Farach noticed how subtle details play a role. In

[1]A **connotation** is an idea that a word makes you think of, apart from its meaning.

Western cultures, he says, "rounded corners are more accepted than in Arabic countries. In typography, Arabs prefer blade-like typefaces …"

E
Sometimes the differences are not so subtle. "The big difference is orientation," says Durado. "Arabs write and read from right to left." This sometimes means inverting, or flipping, images, but this can present challenges. "[N]ot all images can just be flipped," says Durado, citing examples such as maps.

F
Konstantinos Antonopoulos, a Greek designer working for *Al Jazeera English* in Qatar, remarks how different publications within the same company often need different visuals for the same stories. *Al Jazeera Arabic*, for example, "has a strong visual language, spearheaded by the brilliant typography of the Arabic alphabet." But the company may change the visuals for its publications in Turkey or the Balkans, for example. "[They] have their own visual languages," Antonopoulos explains.

The color of money varies around the world.

Graphics director Alberto Lucas López moved from Spain to work for the *South China Morning Post* in Hong Kong. He thinks

G
that some differences in style have to do with Chinese writing. "I could clearly see the parallelism[2] between the Chinese characters and the visual preferences," he says. His

[2] **Parallelism** is a likeness or connection between two or more things.

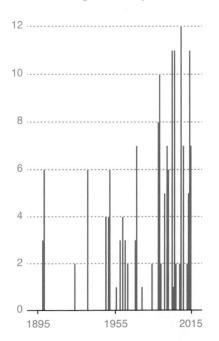

**Months of severe drought**
Palmer Drought Severity Index

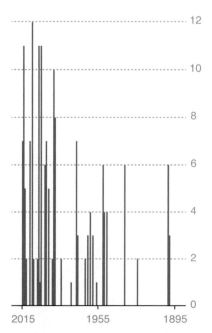

شهور القحط الشديد
مؤشر بالمر لقياس القحط

▲ **The same graph presented in English (left) and Arabic (right) editions of the same publication**

Chinese visuals may be influenced by Chinese writing.

theory is that Chinese visuals are heavily influenced by Chinese writing: complex symbols with many elements compressed in a reduced space. **Nevertheless**, López feels it's important to respect these differences: "Sometimes we see as incorrect what is different from our view of clear structures, strict order, and synthesis. But it's just a different visual culture."

Cultural differences can also influence what gets designed in the first place. Felipe Memoria, a Brazilian designer working in New York, has noticed how sports reporting differs in Brazil and the United States. He speculates that in

contrast to Brazilians, Americans are "really into data." The result: greater **reliance** on infographics—charts, **statistics**, and graphs—in American sports publications.

These journalists and designers have had to adapt, but they're also making their contributions to the cultures they've adopted. Nick Mrozowski, an American designer who worked for many years in Portugal, **emphasizes** the positives of this exchange of ideas. He brought some of his American design preferences to the job, but, he says, "I'm also certain that I absorbed a great deal more from Portugal's talented creatives than I left behind."

# UNDERSTANDING THE READING

**A** Check (✓) the three main ideas of the reading passage.

UNDERSTANDING
MAIN IDEAS

☐ 1. Different cultures use colors to mean different things.

☐ 2. Information should be presented in a visual style that is culturally appropriate.

☐ 3. Today's designers of visual data are struggling to keep up with cultural changes.

☐ 4. People today generally prefer modern infographics to more traditional visual styles.

☐ 5. Cultural differences influence the amount and type of infographics that publications choose to include.

**B** What points do the experts in the passage make? Answer the questions in your own words.

UNDERSTANDING
SUPPORTING IDEAS

1. What does Charles Apple say about the use of the color green?

   _____

2. What does Xan Sabaris point out about the color red?

   _____

3. What challenges about creating visual data do Antonio Farach and Adonis Durado describe?

   _____

4. What does Alberto Lucas López say about the connection between Chinese writing and visual data?

   _____

5. What point does Nick Mrozowski make about his experience in Portugal?

   _____

**C** Work with a partner. Based on the information from the passage, in which publication would you most likely find the following features (1–6)? Why? Discuss with a partner, using evidence from the passage to give reasons.

CRITICAL THINKING:
APPLYING

a. an American publication     b. a Chinese publication     c. an Arabic publication

_____ 1. a diagram where information goes from right to left

_____ 2. a line graph where red shows rising prices

_____ 3. a financial report with green design elements showing profit

_____ 4. graphics with a lot of data packed in a small space

_____ 5. a sports article with a variety of data and infographics

_____ 6. a font style that uses mostly sharp, blade-like edges

**D** Find and underline the following words in **bold** in the reading passage. Use context to identify their meanings. Then match the sentence parts to complete the definitions.

1. Paragraph C: **Deficits** are _____

2. Paragraph E: **Orientation** refers to _____

3. Paragraph E: **Inverting** something means _____

4. Paragraph G: If something is **compressed**, it is _____

5. Paragraph H: If you are **into** something, you are _____

a. losses.

b. very interested in it.

c. pressed tightly together.

d. turning it inside out or upside down.

e. the direction in which something is pointed.

**E** Read the guidelines for selecting charts and graphs for an academic essay. Which do you think are most important? Rank them (1 = most important, 5 = least important). Then work in a group and add two more guidelines that you think are important.

The chart/graph should …

_____ be visually interesting.

_____ use simple typefaces.

_____ be appropriate for your audience.

_____ be based on logical data.

_____ have an objective scale.

Additional guidelines:

_____

_____

**F** Find a magazine or newspaper that is published in your country. Note answers to the questions below. Then discuss them with a partner.

1. What colors are mainly used in this publication? Why do you think this is?

_____

_____

2. List three things you notice about the design in this publication, e.g., the use of text and images, how the elements are arranged, etc. What impact do you think the designer wanted to create through these?

_____

_____

_____

_____

# Writing

## EXPLORING WRITTEN ENGLISH

**A** Match each underlined phrase with the most suitable percentage amount (a–e).

NOTICING

1. The numbers on the vertical axis make it look like Drug A is <u>five times more</u> effective than Drug B.

2. As shown in Figure 1, <u>about a third</u> of the population did not vote.

3. <u>Approximately half</u> the class prefers to take tests on Mondays, as shown in Figure 1.

4. Figure 3 shows that <u>more than a third</u> of the students speak three languages.

5. <u>The majority</u> of the school's students have part-time jobs, as shown in Figure 2.

_____ a. 500 percent

_____ b. 71 percent

_____ c. 38 percent

_____ d. 49.4 percent

_____ e. 33 percent

---

### LANGUAGE FOR WRITING  Describing Visual Information

When you include graphs and charts in an essay, label them sequentially (e.g., Figure 1, Figure 2, etc.) so they are easier to refer to. You can use the following phrases to refer to figures within an essay:

> *Figure 1 shows (that)* …
>
> *As Figure 1 illustrates,* …
>
> *As seen/shown in Figure 1,* …

Note: Use a comma before or after phrases that include *as*.

It can sometimes be easier for your reader to visualize the data if you use words and phrases instead of numbers (e.g., *a quarter* instead of *25 percent*). You can also use modifiers that round up or down important quantities from a chart (e.g., *less than twenty kilos* instead of *19.8 kilos*). Using words and phrases like these can make your message more meaningful and impactful.

Below are some words and phrases that express quantities.

| | | |
|---|---|---|
| *a quarter of* | *a third of* | *two-thirds of* |
| *two-fifths of* | *a half of* | *two times / five times more* |
| *approximately* | *the majority of* | *twice / five times as much* |
| *about* | *almost all* | *less than* |
| *more than* | *nearly* | |

**B** Look at the bar graph below. Then complete the sentences using the words and phrases in the box. One is extra.

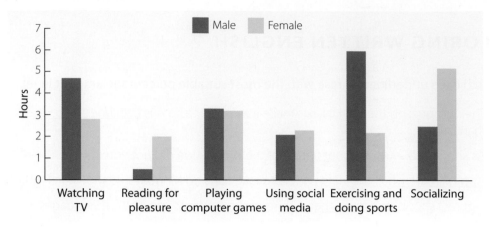

**Figure 1: Time spent on the weekend by 18–24-year-olds**

| half | twice | a third |
| more than | four times | less than |

1. As Figure 1 shows, women read for pleasure _____ as much as men.

2. Men and women spend _____ three hours playing computer games.

3. Women spend almost _____ as much time socializing as men, as seen in Figure 1.

4. Women spend about _____ as much time as men exercising and doing sports, as illustrated in Figure 1.

5. As shown in Figure 1, women watch _____ three hours of TV during the weekend.

**C** Write two more sentences about the graph in exercise B using words and phrases that express quantity.

1. _____

2. _____

**WRITING SKILL** Writing a Persuasive Essay

In a persuasive essay, you choose one side of an issue and persuade your reader to agree with your position. You present your position in your thesis statement and support it with reasons that show why you think it's correct.

The body paragraphs in a persuasive essay should include good reasons and convincing details that show why your position is correct. Convincing details include facts, direct quotes, and data based on evidence.

Charts and graphs that show the data you're referring to can make your arguments even stronger. They make your argument more credible and provide evidence that what you are saying is true. For example, if you are arguing that self-driving cars are more dangerous than traditional cars, a chart or graph that compares accident rates for each type of vehicle will make your argument more convincing.

The topics for your persuasive essay should not be:

- just factual (e.g., *Tigers are an endangered species.*).
- very subjective (e.g., *Tigers are more beautiful than leopards.*).
- too broad (e.g., *Animals should be protected.*).

The thesis statement in a persuasive essay should state your position about the topic. A good thesis statement should focus on a specific part of the topic. Compare these examples of thesis statements.

- *Keeping exotic animals as pets is a bad idea.* [too general]
- *Having exotic animals such as tigers and chimpanzees as pets is harmful for both the animals and the people who keep them.* [more specific]

**D** For each item (1–3), choose the better topic to use in a persuasive essay. Then discuss with a partner why the other topics are not good ones for a persuasive essay.

1. a. High schools should require students to wear uniforms.

   b. Some high schools require students to wear uniforms.

2. a. Socializing in person is more fun than using social media.

   b. Socializing in person is a better way to get to know people than using social media.

3. a. Airports should be made safer than they are now.

   b. Airports should screen passengers before they board planes.

**E** Imagine you are writing a persuasive essay on the topic of "We should eat insects instead of meat and fish." Work with a partner to answer the questions below.

1. Choose the more suitable thesis statement for the topic. Why do you think it's better?

   a. Eating insects is generally better than eating meat and fish.

   b. Eating insects rather than meat and fish is healthier and more environmentally friendly.

2. Check (✔) two reasons that best support the thesis statement.

   ☐ a. Insects are packed with nutrition.

   ☐ b. We need protein in our diets.

   ☐ c. Farmers care more for animals and fish.

   ☐ d. Eating insects produces less waste than eating meat or fish.

3. Check (✔) the four best details to include in the essay's body paragraphs. Why are the other details not as good?

   ☐ a. Only 20 percent of an insect is thrown away.

   ☐ b. More than half of a cow is wasted.

   ☐ c. Eating meat is very wasteful.

   ☐ d. Insects have as much protein as meat and fish.

   ☐ e. Insects have 10 times as much vitamin $B_{12}$ as salmon.

   ☐ f. People from some cultures enjoy eating insects.

# REVISING PRACTICE

The draft below is a persuasive essay about whether people should eat insects rather than meat and fish. Add the sentences (a–c) in the most suitable spaces.

a. As resources become scarce and the global population increases, perhaps someday more people will consider sitting down for a meal of crickets and worms.

b. One reason insects make a good food source is that consuming them produces much less waste than eating meat or fish.

c. As illustrated in Figure 2, crickets have as much protein as salmon, chickens, and cows.

**A**

Does a meal of fried crickets and marinated worms sound tasty to you? While insects are already a desirable source of protein in some parts of the world, they are not very popular worldwide. However, there are good reasons for eating insects instead of meat and fish.

**B**

_____ When we eat chicken or beef, we generally only eat the muscles and throw away the rest. As Figure 1 shows, the majority of a cricket's body can be used as food—only one-fifth is wasted. Conversely, with most other protein sources, such as fish, chicken, and cattle, much more of the animal is wasted. Only about half of a salmon or a chicken is used as food, and less than half of a cow is consumed. This means the majority of the animal's body is thrown away.

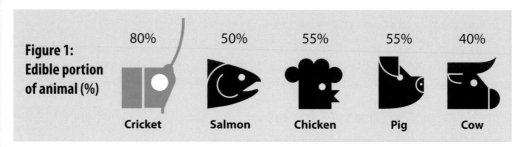

**Figure 1: Edible portion of animal (%)**

| Cricket | Salmon | Chicken | Pig | Cow |
|---------|--------|---------|-----|-----|
| 80% | 50% | 55% | 55% | 40% |

**C**

Another reason we should eat insects is that they are packed with nutrition. Many insects are rich in protein. _____ They also contain much less fat, making them a healthy choice. In addition, insects such as crickets are a good source of vitamins and minerals. They have 10 times as much vitamin $B_{12}$ as salmon, almost five times as much magnesium as beef, and more calcium than milk.

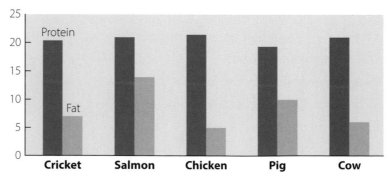

**Figure 2: Nutritional value of animal (%)**

The percent of protein and fat in crickets is similar to that of most meats.

**D**

It's clear that there are benefits to replacing meat and fish with insects. In addition to being less wasteful and equally nutritious, insects are available all over the world and they reproduce rapidly. _____

## EDITING PRACTICE

Read the information below.

When describing visual data, remember to:
- use a comma before or after phrases that include *as* (e.g., *As Figure 2 shows*, …).
- capitalize the "F" in "Figure" when referring to specific graphs or diagrams.
- make sure there is a noun-verb agreement after expressions describing quantity (e.g., *a third of, a quarter of, a majority of*, etc.).

Correct one mistake with language for describing visual data in each of the sentences (1–5).

1. Much of the animal is wasted: less than half are used for food.

2. A quarter of people spends more than four hours a day online.

3. As figure 1 illustrates, approximately a third of the animal is wasted.

4. Two-fifths of the students studies in the school library.

5. As Figure 3 shows more than half of the class prefers to use their phones to take notes.

## UNIT REVIEW

Answer the following questions.

1. What are two things that designers should keep in mind when they create infographics?

   _____

   _____

   _____

2. What are some concession words and phrases that signal counterarguments?

   _____

   _____

   _____

3. Do you remember the meanings of these words? Check (✔) the ones you know. Look back at the unit and review the ones you don't know.

   Reading 1:

   ☐ convey          ☐ deliberately       ☐ downside
   ☐ faulty          ☐ interpret AWL      ☐ misleading
   ☐ neutral AWL     ☐ objective AWL      ☐ stand out
   ☐ vision

   Reading 2:

   ☐ context AWL     ☐ emphasize AWL      ☐ gesture
   ☐ have to do with ☐ nevertheless AWL
   ☐ propose         ☐ publication AWL    ☐ reliance AWL
   ☐ statistic AWL   ☐ universal

An endangered Northern spotted owl, a source of much controversy in logging communities of the Pacific Northwest, rests in a fresh clear-cut near Merlin, Oregon.

**OBJECTIVES** To learn how to write an argument essay
To control tone with modals
To learn to use the *if* clause

*Can you persuade someone to agree with your opinion on nature conservation versus industry growth?*

# What Is an Argument Essay?

In an **argument essay**, the writer's purpose is to persuade the audience to agree with his or her opinion about a controversial topic. In a sociology class, for example, you might write an essay arguing that female military personnel can be as effective as male military personnel in combat missions. In a history class, your essay might try to convince readers that World War I could have been avoided if certain steps had been taken. In an argument essay, sometimes referred to as a **persuasive essay**, the writer states the claim (opinion), gives reasons to support it, and tries to convince the audience that he or she is correct.

## Arguing Pro or Con

Choosing a topic that is appropriate for an argument essay is especially important because some things cannot be argued. For example, you cannot argue that a tulip is more beautiful than a daisy because this is an opinion that cannot be supported by facts. However, you can argue that tulips are more popular than daisies and support the argument with facts about florists' sales of the two kinds of flowers.

Here are a few effective topics and thesis statements for an argument essay:

- Marriage before the age of eighteen:  People under the age of eighteen should not be allowed to marry.

- Standardized testing:  Standardized testing should not be required as part of the application process for a university.

- Fast-food restaurants:  Fast-food restaurants ought to list the calorie counts for all the food that they sell.

You can argue either for (**pro**) or against (**con**) these statements. If your topic does not have two viewpoints, your essay will not be effective. Look at the following example of an ineffective topic and thesis statement.

Jazz music:  Jazz music began with African Americans.

You cannot argue against this statement because it is a fact. Therefore, you cannot write an argument essay using this thesis statement.

# Convincing the Reader

Your job as the writer of an argument essay is to convince your readers that your opinion about a topic (your thesis statement) is the most valid viewpoint. To do this, your essay needs to be balanced—it must include an opposing viewpoint, or **counterargument**. Even though you are arguing one side of an issue (either for or against), you must think about what someone on the other side of the issue would argue. As soon as you give your opponent's point of view, you must offer a **refutation** of it. This means that you refute the other point of view, or show how it is wrong. If you give only your opinion, your essay will sound like propaganda, and your readers will not be convinced of your viewpoint.

### ACTIVITY 1  Studying an Argument Essay

This essay argues the use of school uniforms. Discuss the Preview Questions with a classmate. Then read the example essay and answer the questions that follow.

### Preview Questions

1. Did you wear a uniform when you went to school?

2. Some people believe that children are too materialistic these days. For example, they may be too interested in wearing brand name clothes and shoes. What is your opinion?

# The School Uniform Question

1      Individualism is a **fundamental** part of society in many countries. Most people believe in the right to express their own opinion without fear of punishment. This value, however, is coming under fire in an unlikely place—the **public school** classroom. The issue is school uniforms. Should public school students be allowed to make individual decisions about clothing, or should all students be required to wear a uniform? School uniforms are the better choice for three reasons.

2      First, wearing school uniforms would help make students' lives simpler. They would no longer have to decide what to wear every morning, sometimes trying on outfit after outfit in an effort to choose. Uniforms would not only save time but also would eliminate the stress often associated with this chore.

3      Second, school uniforms influence students to act responsibly in groups and as individuals. Uniforms give students the message that school is a special place for learning. In addition, uniforms create a feeling of unity among students. For example, when students do something as a group, such as attend meetings in the auditorium or eat lunch in the cafeteria, the fact that they all wear the same uniform gives them a sense of community. Even more important, statistics show the positive effects that school uniforms have on violence and **truancy**. According to a recent survey in a large school district in Florida, incidents of school violence dropped by 50 percent, attendance and test scores improved, and student suspensions declined approximately 30 percent after school uniforms were introduced.

4      Finally, school uniforms would help make all the students feel equal. Students' standards of living differ greatly from family to family, and some people are **well-off** while others are not. People sometimes forget that school is a place to get an education, not to promote a "fashion show." **Implementing** mandatory school uniforms would make all the students look the same regardless of their financial status. School uniforms would promote pride and help to raise the self-esteem of students who cannot afford to wear expensive clothing.

5      Opponents of mandatory uniforms say that students who wear school uniforms cannot express their individuality. This point has some merit on the surface. However, as stated previously, school is a place to learn, not to **flaunt** wealth and fashion. Society must decide if individual expression through clothing is more valuable than improved educational performance. It is important to remember that school uniforms would be worn only during school hours. Students can express their individuality in the way that they dress outside of the classroom.

6      In conclusion, there are many well-documented benefits of implementing mandatory school uniforms for students. Studies show that students learn better and act more responsibly when they wear uniforms. Public schools should require uniforms in order to benefit both the students and society as a whole.

**fundamental:** essential, basic

**a public school:** a school run by the state government and paid for by taxes

**truancy:** absence without permission

**well-off:** wealthy

**to implement:** to put into effect

**to flaunt:** to show off, display

## Post-Reading

1. The topic of this essay is school uniforms. What is the hook in the first paragraph?

   _____

   _____

2. What is the thesis statement? _____

   _____

   _____

3. Paragraphs 2, 3, and 4 each give a reason for requiring school uniforms. These reasons can be found in the topic sentence of each paragraph. What are the reasons?

   Paragraph 2: _____

   _____

   Paragraph 3: _____

   _____

   Paragraph 4: _____

   _____

4. In Paragraph 4, what supporting information does the writer give to show that uniforms make students equal?

   _____

   _____

   _____

5. Which paragraph presents a counterargument—an argument that is contrary to, or the opposite of,

   the writer's opinion? _____ What is the counterargument?

   _____

   _____

   _____

6. The writer gives a refutation of the counterargument by showing that it is invalid. What is the writer's refutation?

   _____

   _____

   _____

7. Write the sentence from the concluding paragraph that restates the thesis.

_____

_____

_____

8. Reread the concluding paragraph. What is the writer's opinion about this issue?

_____

_____

_____

# Developing an Argument Essay

## Outlining

**ACTIVITY 2** **Outlining Practice**

The following outline, which is designed for an argument essay, is missing some supporting information. Work with a partner to complete the outline. Use your imagination, knowledge of the topic, and understanding of essay organization to complete this outline with your partner. After you finish, compare your supporting information with other students' work.

**Topic: Mandatory physical education in school**

I. Introduction (Paragraph 1)

Thesis statement: Physical education classes should be required for all public school students in all grades.

II. Body

A. Paragraph 2 (Pro argument 1) topic sentence: Physical education courses promote children's general health.

SUPPORT

1. Researchers have proved that exercise has maximum benefit if done regularly.

2. _____

3. Students should learn the importance of physical fitness at an early age.

B. Paragraph 3 (Pro argument 2) topic sentence: Physical education teaches children transferable life skills.

SUPPORT

1. Kids learn about teamwork while playing team sports.

2. Kids learn about the benefits of healthy competition.

3. _____

C. Paragraph 4 (Pro argument 3) topic sentence: _____

_____

SUPPORT

1. Trained physical education teachers can teach more effectively than parents.

2. Physical education teachers can usually point students toward new and interesting sports.

3. Schools generally have the appropriate facilities and equipment.

D. Paragraph 5 (counterargument and refutation)

SUPPORT

1. Counterargument: Some parents might disagree and claim that only academic subjects should be taught in school.

2. Refutation: Then again, most parents do not have the time or the resources to see to it that their children are getting enough exercise.

III. Conclusion (Paragraph 6) (restated thesis): _____

_____

Physical education has often been downplayed as a minor part of daily school life. If its benefits are taken into account and if schools adopt a 12-year fitness plan, the positive results will foster a new awareness of not only physical fitness but also communication skills.

# Adding Supporting Information

**ACTIVITY 3** **Studying the Supporting Information in an Example Essay**

In this essay, the writer argues about celebrity lifestyles and privacy. Discuss the Preview Questions with a classmate. Then read and study the example essay, and fill in the missing supporting information in the spaces provided.

## Preview Questions

1. Would you like to live the life of a celebrity? What are some of the advantages of being a "star"?

2. List a few famous people who have had difficulty dealing with their celebrity status and lifestyles. Why do you think they had these problems?

## Essay 2

### Privacy for Celebrities

1    The year 1997 will always be remembered as the year of celebrity tragedy. It was the year when Diana, Princess of Wales was killed in a horrific car accident. For weeks, reporters discussed who was at fault. Yes, her chauffeur was driving at an extremely high speed, but the car was being chased by the **paparazzi**. Many people decided that Princess Diana was a victim of these overly aggressive photographers. Was she? Or was it understood that celebrity status came with the compromise of little or no privacy? The debate on celebrity privacy continues, and it seems that almost everyone has an opinion. For many, the concept is simple: privacy ends when celebrity status is achieved. The stars know this, and they need to stop complaining about it.

**the paparazzi:** celebrity photographers

**2**     Being followed and **harassed** should not be a surprise as it is an expected part of being a celebrity.

_____

_____

_____

_____

**to be harassed:** to be bothered by someone

**3**     The media is basically in charge of a person's celebrity status; no media attention equals no stardom.

_____

_____

_____

_____

**4**     Celebrities are often role models, so they need to be prepared for the paparazzi's cameras at all times.

_____

_____

_____

_____

**5**     Some people say that even the most famous people need their privacy, especially in tragic situations. However, celebrity status does not come with the option of choosing the best time to be photographed or followed. Stars knew about the effects of stardom, such as lack of privacy, before they became famous, so they must take the good with the bad.

_____

_____

_____

_____

**6**     Once an actor, singer, or athlete becomes famous, the notion of being a **reluctant** star does not make sense. In essence, celebrities **give up** their privacy the minute they achieve stardom. As responsible members of society, they need to embrace this part of their celebrity status in the same way that they embrace fame, fortune, and **adoration** from their fans.

**reluctant:** unwilling

**to give up:** to surrender, agree not to own

**the adoration:** high regard, worship

# Choosing a Topic

**ACTIVITY 4** **Writing Pro and Con Thesis Statements**

Read the following list of topics for argument essays. For each topic, write a pro (for) thesis statement and a con (against) thesis statement related to the topic. Then compare your statements with your classmates' statements. The first one has been done for you.

1. **Topic: Women in the military**

   Pro thesis statement: _In a society where women are chief executive officers of_ _companies, leaders of nations, and family breadwinners, there is no reason_ _why they should not play an active role in the military._

   Con thesis statement: _Women should not be allowed to fight in the military because_ _they do not have the strength or endurance required in combat._

2. **Topic: Using animals in disease research**

   Pro thesis statement: _____

   _____

   Con thesis statement: _____

   _____

3. **Topic: Driver's license age restrictions**

   Pro thesis statement: _____

   _____

   Con thesis statement: _____

   _____

4. **Topic: Space exploration**

   Pro thesis statement: _____

   _____

   Con thesis statement: _____

   _____

5. **Topic: Internet privacy**

   Pro thesis statement: _____

   _____

   Con thesis statement: _____

   _____

# Grammar for Writing

## Controlling Tone with Modals

In argument essays, good writers are aware of how their arguments sound. Are they too strong? Not strong enough? Certain words can help control the tone of your argument.

**Modals** can change the tone of a sentence. Modals such as *must* and *had better* make a verb stronger. Other modals such as *may, might, should, can,* and *could* make a verb softer. Remember to use modals to strengthen or soften your verbs.

### Asserting a Point

Strong modals such as *must* and *had better* help writers to assert their main points. When you use these words, readers know where you stand on an issue.

**Examples:**

The facts clearly show that researchers **must** stop unethical animal testing.

People who value their health **had better** stop smoking now.

### Acknowledging an Opposing Point

Weaker modals such as *may, might, could, can,* and *would* help writers make an opposing opinion sound weak. You acknowledge an opposing point when you use *may,* for example, but this weak modal shows that the statement is not strong and can be refuted more easily. In short, the use of *may* and *might* is crucial to constructing a proper refutation and then counterargument.

Here is an example from the essay in Activity 2 (page 31):

Some parents **might** disagree and claim that only academic subjects should be taught in school. Then again, most parents do not have the time or the resources to see to it that their children are getting enough exercise.

**Other Examples:**

While it **may** be true that people have eaten meat for a long time, the number one killer of Americans now is heart disease, caused in part by the consumption of large amounts of animal fat.

Some citizens **may** be against mandatory military service, but those who do serve in the military often have a strong sense of pride and personal satisfaction.

Read the following argument essay. Circle the modal in parentheses that you feel is more appropriate.

## Essay 3

### Issues in Morality

1      In order to become a member of the European Union (EU), a country must prove that it handles human rights in a humane and civil way. One major concern of the EU is the death penalty. In fact, the death penalty is not allowed in any of the EU countries. To that end, those countries that want membership must prove that their laws protect the human lives of even the cruelest of criminals. This point of view, however, is not shared by all. Countries such as Singapore, Japan, South Korea, and the United States allow for the death penalty. In fact, the death penalty should be allowed in all countries.

2      The first reason for allowing the death penalty is for the **sake** of punishment itself. Most people agree that criminals who commit serious crimes (**1.** might / should) be separated from society. The punishment (**2.** will / ought to) depend on the degree of the crime.

**sake:** benefit, well being

The death penalty, the most severe form of punishment, ends criminals' lives. It seems reasonable that this **severe** punishment be reserved for those who commit the most serious of crimes.

**severe:** harsh, strict

3    The second reason to allow for the death penalty is financial. The government (**3.** should / will) not have to spend a lot of money on criminals. Next to a death sentence, the most severe punishment is a life sentence in prison, where the government (**4.** might / has to) take care of criminals until they die naturally. These criminals do not actively improve society, but society must provide them free housing and food. It is unfair to use a country's taxes for such a purpose.

4    Finally, one must look at the government and its **role** in society. Society agrees that government has **legitimate** power to make, judge, and carry out the laws; as a result, it (**5.** may / should) also have the power to decide if criminals should die. The death penalty is like any other sentence. If one believes that the government has the right to charge a fine or put criminals into jail, then the government (**6.** could / must) also have the same power to decide the fate of a prisoner's life.

**role:** position, function

**legitimate:** legal, lawful

5    The opponents of the death penalty (**7.** must / might) say that nobody has the right to decide who should die, including the government. However, when the government sends soldiers into war, in some way, it is deciding those soldiers' fate; some will live, and some will be killed. As long as the government makes decisions to send its citizens to the battlefield, it has a right to put criminals to death.

6    There are many good reasons to allow for the death penalty. Certainly not every criminal (**8.** can / should) be put to death. Still, capital punishment (**9.** ought to / will) be viewed as the harshest form of punishment. If no alternate punishment (**10.** can / should) reform a murderer, then capital punishment is the best thing that can be done for that person and for society. Europe has gotten it wrong.

# Counterargument and Refutation

The key technique to persuading the reader that your viewpoint is valid is to support it in every paragraph. While this is not a problem in the first few paragraphs of your essay the **counterargument** goes against your thesis statement. Consequently, every counterargument that you include in your essay needs a refutation. A **refutation** is a response to the counterargument that disproves it.

For example, imagine that you are having an argument with a friend about your topic. She disagrees with your opinion. What do you think will be her strongest argument against your point of view? How will you respond to this counterargument? Your answer is your refutation.

Look at the following excerpts from two argument essays in this unit. The counterarguments are in *italics* and the refutations are underlined.

**From Essay 1:**

> *Opponents of mandatory uniforms say that students who wear school uniforms cannot express their individuality. This point has some merit on the surface.* However, as stated previously school is a place to learn, not to flaunt wealth and fashion.

**From Essay 2:**

> *Some people say that even the most famous people need their privacy, especially in tragic situations.* However, celebrity status does not come with the option of choosing the best time to be photographed or followed. Stars knew about the effects of stardom, for example, lack of privacy, before they became famous, so they must take the good with the bad.

As you can see, what begins as a counterargument ends up as another reason in support of your opinion.

## ACTIVITY 6  Writing a Refutation

Read each counterargument. Then write a one-line refutation. Remember to use a contrasting connection word to begin your refutation.

1. Parents of extremely young beauty pageant contestants believe that these competitive contests help build their children's confidence.

_____

_____

_____

_____

2. A majority of health insurance companies do not provide financial coverage for preventive wellness activities like nutrition management classes or gym memberships, stating that they are too costly to manage.

_____

_____

_____

_____

**3.** Opponents of the fast-food ban in high schools insist that students should have the freedom to eat whatever they wish.

_____

_____

_____

_____

# Avoiding Faulty Logic

Good writers want to convince readers to agree with their arguments—their reasons and conclusions. If your arguments are not logical, you will not persuade your readers. Logic can help prove your point and disprove your opponent's point—and perhaps change your reader's mind about an issue. If you use faulty logic (logic not based on fact), readers will not believe you or take your position seriously.

This section presents a few logical errors that writers sometimes make in argument essays. Try to avoid these errors in your writing.

## *Events Related Only by Sequence*

When one event happens, it does not necessarily cause a second event to happen, even if one follows the other in time.

**Example:**　Henry went to the football game, and then he had a car accident. Therefore, football games cause car accidents.

**Problem:**　The two events may have happened in that order, but do not mislead the reader into thinking that the first action was responsible for the second.

## *Appeal to Authority*

Using famous names may often help you prove or disprove your point. However, be sure to use the name logically and in the proper context.

**Example:**　Beyoncé is a good singer. As a result, she would make a good judge of orchestra conductors.

**Problem:**　While Beyoncé may be a good singer, this quality will not necessarily make her a good judge of orchestra conductors.

## *Sweeping Generalizations*

Words such as *all, always,* and *never* are too broad and cannot be supported.

**Example:**　Everyone is interested in improving the quality of education.

**Problem:**　Really? Everyone? What about a 90-year-old woman who does not have enough money to pay for her medicine? Her immediate concerns are probably not on improving education. She wants her medicine.

### Hasty Generalizations (Insufficient Statistics)

Hasty generalizations are just what they sound like—making quick judgments based on inadequate or not enough information. This kind of logical fallacy is a common error in argument writing.

**Example:** A woman is driving through a small town. She passes three cars, all of which are white pickup trucks. She then writes in her report describing the town that everyone in this town drives a white pickup truck.

**Problem:** The woman only saw three vehicles. The town actually has over 100 cars. The number of cars that she saw was too small for her to come to that conclusion.

### Loaded Words

Some words contain positive or negative connotations. Try to avoid them when you make an argument. Your readers may think you are trying to appeal to them by using these emotionally packed words. In fact, you want to persuade the reader by using logical arguments, not emotional rants.

**Example:** The blue-flag freedom fighters won the war against the green-flag guerrillas.

**Problem:** The terms *freedom fighters* (positive) and *guerrillas* (negative) may influence the readers' opinion about the two groups without any support for the bias.

### Either/Or Arguments

When you argue a point, be careful not to limit the outcome choices to only two or three. In fact, there are often a multitude of choices. When you offer only two scenarios, you are essentially trying to frighten the reader into your beliefs.

**Example:** The instructor must either return the tests or dismiss the class.

**Problem:** This statement implies that only two choices are available to the instructor.

---

**ACTIVITY 7** **Faulty Logic**

Read the following paragraph, and underline all the uses of faulty logic. Write the kind of error each one is above the words.

## Paragraph 1

### Penny Wise

Next week, our fine upstanding citizens will go to the polls to vote for or against a penny sales tax for construction of a new stadium. This law, if passed, will cause extreme hardship for local residents. Our taxes are high enough as it is, so why do our city's apathetic leaders think that we will run happily to the polls and vote "yes"? If we take a look at what happened to our sister city as a result of a similar bill, we will see that this new tax will have negative effects. Last year, that city raised its sales tax by one percent. Only three weeks later, the city was nearly destroyed by a riot in the streets. If we want to keep our fair city as it is, we must either vote "no" on the ballot question or live in fear of violence.

# Grammar for Writing

## Using the *if* Clause

In this section, you will work on one specific type of adverb clause, the *if* clause. *If* clauses explain a condition that is necessary for a specific outcome. Study the following examples:

| Time | *If* Clause / Situation | Outcome |
|------|------------------------|---------|
| General | If it **is** too hot, | we **turn on** the air conditioning. |
| Future | If it **is** too hot, | we **will turn on** the air conditioning. <br> we **can turn on** the air conditioning. <br> we **may turn on** the air conditioning. <br> we **might turn on** the air conditioning. |
| Present | If the restaurant **opened** at noon, (The restaurant does not open at noon.) | we **could eat** lunch there. <br> we **would eat** lunch there. <br> we **might eat** lunch there. |
| Past | If the students **had asked** questions during the lecture, (They did not ask questions during the lecture.) | they **would have understood** the concepts better. <br> they **might have understood** the concepts better. <br> they **could have understood** the concepts better. |

### ACTIVITY 8  Identifying and Labeling *if* Clauses

The following sentences were taken from this unit. Each sentence contains an *if* clause. Underline the verbs in both parts of the sentence. In the space provided, identify the *if* clause as either past (P), present (PR), or future (F) conditional.

_____ 1. If we believe that the government has the right to put criminals into jail, then the government should also have the same power to decide the fate of a prisoner's life.

_____ 2. If no punishment can reform a murderer, then the death penalty is the best thing that can be done for that person and for society.

_____ 3. If we want to keep our fair city as it is, we must either vote "no" on the ballot question or live in fear of violence.

_____ 4. If schools adopt a 12-year fitness plan, the positive results will foster a new awareness of not only physical fitness but also communication skills.

_____ 5. Researchers have proved that exercise has maximum benefit if it is done regularly.

_____ 6. World War I could have been avoided if certain steps had been taken.

_____ 7. If this law is passed, it will cause extreme hardship for local residents.

# Original Student Writing: Argument Essay

## Brainstorming

**Brainstorming** will help you get started with your argument essay. In this section, you will choose any method of brainstorming that works for you and develop supporting information.

**ACTIVITY 11** Choosing a Topic

Follow the steps below to develop ideas for an argument essay.

1. First, choose a thesis statement from the statements that you wrote in Activity 4 on pages 34–35 or choose any other topic and thesis statement that you want to write about. Remember that the topic must have more than one point of view to qualify as an argument.

   Essay topic: _____

   Thesis statement: _____

   _____

2. Now brainstorm ideas about your topic. Write everything you can think of that supports your argument. You may want to begin by answering this question about your thesis statement: *Why do I believe this?*

3. Look at your brainstorming information again. Choose three or four reasons that support your thesis most effectively and circle them. You now know what your major supporting information will be.

4. Now that you have written your thesis statement and a few reasons to support it, it is time to give attention to opposing points of view. On the lines below, write one counterargument and a refutation for your argument essay.

   Counterargument: _____

   _____

   _____

   Refutation: _____

   _____

   _____

5. Remember to include a restatement of your thesis and your opinion about the issue in your conclusion.

If you need ideas for words and phrases, see the Useful Vocabulary for Better Writing on pages 116–119.

Complete the following outline as a guide to help you brainstorm a more detailed plan for your argument essay. Use your ideas from Activity 11. You may need to use either more or fewer points under each heading. Write complete sentences where possible.

**Topic:** _____

1. Introduction (Paragraph 1)

   **A.** Hook: _____

   **B.** Connecting information: _____

   _____

   **C.** Thesis statement: _____

   _____

2. Body

   **A.** Paragraph 2 (first reason) topic sentence: _____

   _____

   SUPPORT

   1. _____

   2. _____

   3. _____

   **B.** Paragraph 3 (second reason) topic sentence: _____

   _____

   SUPPORT

   1. _____

   2. _____

   3. _____

   **C.** Paragraph 4 (third reason) topic sentence: _____

   _____

   SUPPORT

   1. _____

   2. _____

   3. _____

**D.** Paragraph 5 (counterargument and refutation)

    **1.** Counterargument: _____

    _____

    **2.** Refutation: _____

    _____

**3.** Conclusion (Paragraph 6)

    **A.** Restated thesis:

    _____

    _____

    **B.** Opinion:

    _____

    _____

### ACTIVITY 13  Peer Editing Your Outline

Exchange books with a partner and look at Activity 12. Read your partner's outline. Then use Peer Editing Sheet 1 on ELTNGL.com/sites/els to help you comment on your partner's outline. Be sure to offer positive suggestions and comments that will help your partner improve his or her writing. Consider your partner's comments as you revise your outline. Make sure you have enough information to develop your supporting sentences.

### ACTIVITY 14  Writing an Argument Essay

Write an argument essay based on your revised outline from Activity 12. Use at least two of the vocabulary words or phrases presented in Activities 8 and 9. Underline these words and phrases in your essay. Be sure to refer to the seven steps in the writing process in the *Brief Writer's Handbook* on pages 91–97.

### ACTIVITY 15  Peer Editing Your Essay

Exchange papers from Activity 14 with a partner. Read your partner's essay. Then use Peer Editing Sheet 2 on ELTNGL.com/sites/els to help you comment on your partner's writing. Be sure to offer positive suggestions and comments that will help your partner improve his or her essay. Consider your partner's comments as you revise your own essay.

# Additional Topics for Writing

Here are more ideas for topics for an argument essay. Before you write, be sure to refer to the seven steps in the writing process in the *Brief Writer's Handbook*, pages 91–97.

**PHOTO**
**TOPIC:** Look at the photograph on pages 24–25. Is the growth of industry more important than nature conservation? Make a decision about this issue, and write an argument essay about industry versus nature.

**TOPIC 2:** At what age should a person be considered an adult? Make a decision about this issue and then argue your point of view. Do not forget to include a counterargument and refutation.

**TOPIC 3:** Is technology (television, computers, cell phones, tablet devices, MP3 players) beneficial for children under the age of five? Should a child be allowed to have full access to technology before the age of five? Develop a thesis statement about some aspect of the age limit for technology issue and support it in your argument essay.

**TOPIC 4:** Should a passing score on an English achievement test be the main requirement for international students to enter a university in an English-speaking country? What are the pros and cons of this issue? Choose one side and write your essay in support of it.

**TOPIC 5:** The media often place heavy emphasis on the opinions and actions of celebrities, such as actors and sports stars. Should we pay attention to these opinions and actions? Are they important or not? Choose one side of this argument and write your essay in support of it.

# Timed Writing

How quickly can you write in English? There are many times when you must write quickly, such as on a test. It is important to feel comfortable during those times. Timed-writing practice can make you feel better about writing quickly in English.

1. Take out a piece of paper.
2. Read the essay guidelines and the writing prompt.
3. Write a basic outline, including the thesis and your three main points.
4. Write a five-paragraph essay.
5. You have 40 minutes to write your essay.

**Argument Essay Guidelines**

- Be sure to include a counterargument and a refutation.
- Remember to give your essay a title.
- Double-space your essay.
- Write as legibly as possible (if you are not using a computer).
- Select an appropriate principle of organization for your topic.
- Include a short introduction (with a thesis statement), body paragraphs, and a conclusion.
- Try to give yourself a few minutes before the end of the activity to review your work. Check for spelling, verb tense, and subject–verb agreement mistakes.

*What should happen to students who are caught cheating on an exam? Why?*

**NOTES**

# WORLD LANGUAGES 3

The Sign Post Forest in Watson Lake, Canada, has more than 70,000 signs from around the world.

## THINK AND DISCUSS

1 How many languages do you speak? How well do you speak them?

2 What are the most common languages in your country?

# Reading 1

## PREPARING TO READ

**A** The words and phrases in **blue** below are used in Reading 1. Read the paragraph. Then match the correct form of each word or phrase to its definition.

Why should you learn a second language? **Acquiring** another language can **lead to** many opportunities in life, both professional and personal. For example, many employers regard **competence** in a second language as a desirable quality in job seekers, and experts **anticipate** this trend to continue to grow. People who speak only their **native** language may be seen as less valuable. In addition, international travel can be more rewarding for people who can speak the languages of the places they are visiting, as it allows them to have conversations with locals and to make new friends. **Furthermore**, speaking more than one language can **expand** a person's cognitive abilities. For example, research shows that multilingual people have better memories and better problem-solving skills.

1. _____ (v) to result in

2. _____ (v) to get something

3. _____ (adv) in addition

4. _____ (n) the ability to do something well

5. _____ (v) to make larger in size or scale

6. _____ (v) to foresee or expect something

7. _____ (adj) connected to a person's place of birth

**B** Discuss these questions with a partner.

1. What do you think are the best ways to **acquire** a new language?

2. What other opportunities can learning a second language **lead to**?

**C** Work with a partner. Discuss your answers to these questions.

1. Why do you think English is so commonly used today?

2. Do you think English will be as important in 50 years? Why or why not?

**D** Read the title and subheadings, and look at the photos in the reading passage. What do you think it is about? Check your idea as you read.

a. the role of English and other languages in the future

b. evidence that English will be less commonly spoken in the future

c. reasons why English has become a global language for communication

▲ **Over a billion people worldwide are learning English.**

# THE FUTURE OF ENGLISH

🎧 Track 3

A

The world's language system is at a crossroads, and a new **linguistic** order is about to emerge. That is the conclusion of a study authored by David Graddol, a researcher on the future of language. He argues that this transformation is partly due to demographics. The world's population rose quickly during the second half of the 20th century, and much of this increase took place in developing countries. This has had an impact on the world's top languages.

B

In his study, Graddol points out that there has been a relative decline in the use of English as a first language. In the mid-20th century, people who spoke English as a first language **constituted** about 9 percent of the world's population. By 2050, the figure is expected to be just 5 percent. Currently, English still has the third largest number of **native** speakers, with Arabic and Hindi lagging **considerably** behind in fourth and fifth places. However, these two languages are expected to catch up by around 2050. Even so, they are not the fastest growing languages; some other languages such as Bengali (spoken in Bangladesh and India), Tamil (spoken in Sri Lanka and India), and Malay (spoken in parts of Southeast Asia) are experiencing even faster growth.

# UNDERSTANDING THE READING

UNDERSTANDING
MAIN IDEAS

**A** Match the paragraphs (A–G) to their main ideas.

_____ 1. As the world becomes increasingly multilingual, monolinguals will need to learn to adapt.

_____ 2. The use of English is growing in the world of science.

_____ 3. Knowledge of multiple languages will be an essential skill in future workplaces.

_____ 4. Population changes are having an important effect on the world's language system.

_____ 5. Other languages besides English will become equally widespread, but there may not be a single global language.

_____ 6. English for science will expand because the field is contributing new words and expressions to the language.

_____ 7. The number of native English speakers is decreasing, while the number of native speakers of other languages is growing.

UNDERSTANDING
DETAILS

**B** Scan the passage to find answers to the questions below.

1. Where did the world's population increase the most in the second half of the 20th century?

   _____

2. What are three of the most rapidly growing languages?

   _____

3. Why is the dominance of one language useful in science?

   _____

4. What language is increasingly becoming an important business language? Why?

   _____

INFERRING MEANING

**C** Find and underline the following words and expressions in **bold** in the reading passage. Use context to identify their meanings. Then complete the definitions.

1. Paragraph A: **Demographics** relates to the characteristics of _____.
   a. human populations
   b. language change

2. Paragraph B: If something is **lagging** behind, it is _____.
   a. getting close
   b. moving slowly

3. Paragraph B: If a person or thing **catches up**, they _____.
   a. take something away from someone or something else
   b. reach the same point as someone or something else

4. Paragraph C: If something **dominates** in an area, it is the most _____.
   a. well-known
   b. common or important

**D** Look back at the graph in the reading passage. Note answers to these questions and discuss with a partner.

INTERPRETING VISUAL INFORMATION

1. Which language has the greatest number of first-language speakers? Which has the second greatest number of native speakers?

   _____

2. Which language has the greatest number of second language speakers?

   _____

3. Which two languages have more non-native speakers than native speakers? What does this show about these languages?

   _____

   _____

> **CRITICAL THINKING** **Applying an idea to a real-world situation** means comparing situations that you read about to experiences in your own life. Ask yourself: How do the ideas in the text relate to my experience—are they similar or different? Do I agree or disagree with what the author is saying? Do the ideas in the text change my opinions about anything?

**E** Think about the ideas in the reading passage and discuss these questions with a partner.

CRITICAL THINKING: APPLYING IDEAS

1. What is the main reason you are studying English? Is your reason similar to or different from the reasons described in the reading passage?

   _____

   _____

2. Do you think that it is important for people in your country to learn more than one second language? Why or why not? Note two reasons.

   _____

   _____

# DEVELOPING READING SKILLS

> **READING SKILL** Understanding Predictions
>
> Different words and phrases, such as *definitely* and *maybe*, indicate a writer's level of certainty about a statement. Similarly, when you read about a prediction, look for words and expressions that express the writer's degree of certainty. Ask yourself: Which predictions does the writer feel certain about? Which ones do they feel less certain about?
>
> Writers use the modal *will* to make predictions that they are most certain about.
> > *In the near future, students **will** study Mandarin as a second language.*
>
> They use words such as *expect*, *anticipate*, *believe*, and *likely* to make predictions that they are reasonably certain about.
> > *Educators **expect** that the number of students learning English will decline.*
> > *We **anticipate** that there will be fewer students next semester.*
>
> When writers are less certain about a prediction, they use words such as *seem* and *probably*. The modals *may, might,* and *could* indicate even less certainty.
> > *English will **probably** continue to be an important language in business.*
> > *Mandarin **might** replace English as the most popular second language in my school.*

IDENTIFYING
PREDICTIONS

**A**  Find an example of these predictions in the passage. Then write the word that the author uses to express a level of certainty.

1.  an example of a reasonably certain prediction in paragraph E  _____

2.  an example of a less certain prediction in paragraph F  _____

ANALYZING
PREDICTIONS

**B**  Answer these questions about other predictions in the passage.

1.  Look for and underline the four predictions described below in the reading passage.

    a.  which language dominates in the future            _____

    b.  when English as a global language reaches its peak    _____

    c.  businesses whose employees speak only one language   _____

    d.  monolinguals in a multilingual society           _____

2.  How certain does the author feel about each prediction above? Rate them (1 = less certain, 2 = reasonably certain, 3 = certain) and discuss your answers with a partner.

3.  Do you disagree with any of the predictions above? Why? Note your ideas and discuss with a partner.

_____

_____

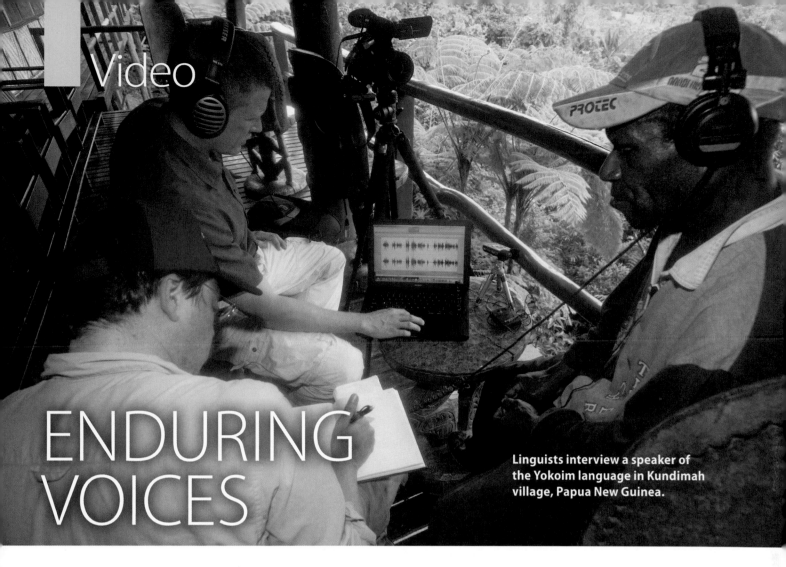

Video

# ENDURING VOICES

Linguists interview a speaker of the Yokoim language in Kundimah village, Papua New Guinea.

## BEFORE VIEWING

**A** Look at the photo and read the caption. What are the researchers doing? Why do you think they are doing this? Discuss with a partner.

PREDICTING

**B** Read the information about the Living Tongues Institute. Then answer the questions.

LEARNING ABOUT THE TOPIC

Half of the world's 7,000 languages may disappear in the next few decades, but linguists from the Living Tongues Institute are working hard to save them and the important historical and cultural information they contain. In one town in India, researchers observed that the younger generation was not speaking the traditional language of their parents. Young people tend to use global languages such as English or Hindi.

1. Why is the Living Tongues Institute trying to save dying languages?

   _____

2. Why do you think the younger generation in that Indian town is no longer speaking the traditional language?

   _____

**C** The words in **bold** below are used in the video. Read the sentences. Then match the correct form of each word to its definition.

> Young people are **abandoning** the languages of their parents and speaking more dominant languages.
>
> When people no longer use a language, language **extinction** occurs.
>
> India has great linguistic **diversity**—it has more than 22 official languages.
>
> If people **neglect** their native languages, the languages will eventually be forgotten.

1. _____ (n) a variety

2. _____ (v) to not give attention to

3. _____ (v) to give up something completely

4. _____ (n) a situation in which something no longer exists

## WHILE VIEWING

**A** ▶ Watch the video. Complete the summary with suitable words.

The Enduring Voices project was created to bring attention to the issue of language loss around the world. In [1]_____, linguists on the team spoke with a man who is probably [2]_____ of his language. The team then went to the village of Hong in northeast India, where it collected information on Apatani—a language now mostly used by [3]_____. The team hopes that by creating a [4]_____ of these dying languages, it is able to keep them alive.

**B** ▶ Watch the video again. Circle T for true, F for false, or NG if the information is not given.

1. Northeast India is a language hot spot.      **T   F   NG**

2. Younger people in Hong prefer to speak in English and Hindi      **T   F   NG**
   because they want to move out of the village.

3. Only one speaker of Apatani is left in the village of Hong.      **T   F   NG**

4. The team taught the villagers how to use the technology kit      **T   F   NG**
   so they can continue to keep a record of their traditional language.

## AFTER VIEWING

**A** Do you think recording the words and phrases of a language is enough to keep it alive? Why or why not? Discuss with a partner.

**B** Does the language trend shown in the video support the predictions about language in Reading 1? Why or why not? Discuss with a partner.

# Reading 2

## PREPARING TO READ

**A** The words and phrases in **blue** below are used in Reading 2. Complete the sentences with the correct words and phrases. Use a dictionary to help you.

| | | | | |
|---|---|---|---|---|
| combined | critically | died out | express | rate |
| roughly | highly | political | rapidly | perspective |

1. The total number of native speakers of Mandarin Chinese currently exceeds the _____ number of native English speakers and Arabic speakers.

2. According to a 2015 study, the current _____ of species extinction is _____ 100 times higher than in the past; within this century, at least a dozen species have _____ completely.

3. Conservationists are working to preserve the last Sumatran tigers as there are fewer than 700 left in the wild. The species is _____ endangered.

4. According to a 2014 study, the ability to _____ yourself in French will become a _____ valued skill for anyone doing business in Africa. This is because the population of French-speaking people in sub-Saharan Africa is expected to grow _____ in the coming decades.

5. From one _____, it is an advantage if everyone in the world speaks the same language; another viewpoint is that it will reduce cultural diversity.

6. The status of languages can be influenced by _____ decisions, such as when governments choose to promote or ban minority languages in schools.

**B** Discuss these questions with a partner.
   1. Aside from speaking and writing, how else do people **express** themselves?
   2. If you want to learn a new language **rapidly**, what should you do?

**C** Look at the questions in the three headings of the reading passage. Note some possible answers for each one and share with a partner. Then check your ideas as you read.

_____

_____

_____

# VANISHING VOICES

Johnny Hill, Jr. is one of the last speakers of Chemehuevi, an endangered Native American language.

🎧 Track 4

A  The Earth's population of seven billion people speaks roughly 7,000 languages. However, there is a very unequal distribution in the number of people who speak these languages. In fact, just 85 of them are spoken by 78 percent of the world's population. And the least common 3,500 languages are spoken by fewer than 9 million people combined. For example, there are only 235,000 speakers of Tuvan, the native language of the Republic of Tuva in the Russian Federation. And there are fewer than 2,000 known speakers of Aka, a language from Arunachal Pradesh in northeastern India.

B  Many of these smaller languages are disappearing rapidly. More than 1,000 are listed as critically or severely endangered. In fact, it is estimated that a language "dies" every 14 days. According to linguists, within the next century, nearly half of the world's current languages will disappear as communities abandon native tongues in favor of English, Mandarin, or Spanish. But should we be concerned about language extinction? And what can we do to prevent it?

## HOW DO LANGUAGES DIE?

C  Since humans first started to communicate with each other, languages have come and gone. The languages of powerful groups have spread, while the languages of smaller cultures have disappeared. Today, languages dominate not only because they are spoken by powerful groups, but also because of how they are used. For example, languages like English are commonly used on television, on the Internet, and in international business.

In an increasingly globalized age, languages spoken in remote places are no longer protected from dominant world languages. Languages such as Mandarin, English, Russian, Hindi, Spanish, and Arabic reach into tiny communities and compete with smaller languages. When one language dominates, children from nondominant language groups tend to lose their native languages as they grow up,

D go to school, and get jobs. Sometimes they don't want to speak the less dominant languages, partly because they think that speaking these languages makes it difficult to succeed. These attitudes, along with the strong desire to fit in, threaten the survival of native languages. **Political** pressure can also affect the survival of smaller languages. Governments sometimes pass laws that require people to use dominant languages at school, at work, and in the media.

## WHY SHOULD WE BE CONCERNED?

Why is the extinction of a language with a small number of speakers a concern? Different languages express unique perspectives on the world. For example, languages can show us how a culture experiences basic concepts such as time, numbers, and colors. The Pirahã, an Amazonian tribe, appear to have no words

E for numbers. Instead, they get by with quantity words such as *few* and *many*. This suggests that numbers may be an invention of culture, and not an idea that humans are born with. The way that people think of colors also depends on their language. For example, the Candoshi language in Peru uses one word to describe shades of green, blue, and purple. However, it has a separate word for dark green.

The loss of a language also means the loss of knowledge, similar to the possibility of losing a future miracle drug[1] if a species **dies out**. For example, the Seri in the Sonoran Desert of Mexico have terms for more than 300 desert plants.

F By studying their language, scientists learned about a **highly** nutritious[2] food source similar to wheat, called *eelgrass*. Scientists have also learned a lot about the habitats and behaviors of local animals. There are only 650 to 1,000 Seri speakers left, so by losing the language we might lose important scientific knowledge.

[1] A **miracle drug** is a treatment for a disease that is surprisingly effective and safe.
[2] Something that is **nutritious** is healthy.

### Language Hot Spots

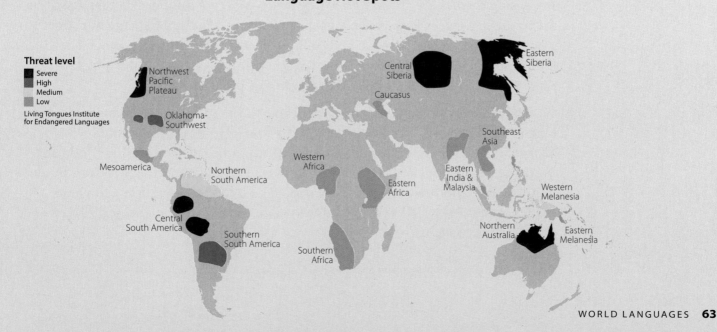

The Seri have more than 50 terms for family relationships, such as between two cousins.

G  If languages continue to vanish at today's rapid rate, we may lose knowledge about plants that could someday lead to useful drugs. We may also lose information about the history and skills of many of the world's cultures. In Micronesia, for example, some sailors can find their way across miles of ocean without using any maps or modern equipment. Sadly, their skills and knowledge are encoded in languages that are at risk of disappearing.

## HOW CAN WE SAVE DYING LANGUAGES?

H  Fortunately, groups around the world are working to bring threatened languages back to life. These groups are giving people more opportunity to use these threatened languages, and are changing the attitudes that caused people to stop using them. One group that is helping to preserve disappearing languages is the Enduring Voices Project. This project works to identify language hot spots—places with languages that are both unique and at risk of disappearing. The Enduring Voices Project has two goals: to accurately document the languages of these places and to record the cultural information they contain.

I  Projects such as these are very important to the survival of endangered languages. The work of these groups will allow us to pass on a wealth of historical, cultural, and scientific knowledge to future generations. As Enduring Voices team member K. David Harrison says, it would be wrong for us to think that "we have nothing to learn from people who just a generation ago were hunter-gatherers[3] … What they know—which we've forgotten or never knew—may someday save us."

[3] **Hunter-gatherers** are people who live by hunting and collecting food rather than by farming.

# UNDERSTANDING THE READING

**A** Choose the main idea of each section in the reading passage.

UNDERSTANDING MAIN IDEAS

1. **How Do Languages Die?**
   a. It's difficult for less dominant languages to spread and grow because their speakers often live in areas that are more remote.
   b. A greater number of people today are choosing to speak widely used languages such as English and Mandarin over their native languages.

2. **Why Should We Be Concerned?**
   a. When a language disappears, we lose knowledge and culture that is specific to that language.
   b. Scientists believe that information from speakers of smaller languages can help them find a miracle drug.

3. **How Can We Save Dying Languages?**
   a. Some groups are encouraging the use of minority languages and recording them.
   b. Some groups are building centers that teach minority languages to younger generations of speakers.

**B** Look back at the reading passage to find answers to the questions below.

UNDERSTANDING DETAILS

1. What do linguists predict will happen to the world's languages in the next 100 years? Why?

   _____

2. What are three factors that contribute to the death of languages?

   _____

   _____

3. Why is the work done by the Enduring Voices Project important? Give one reason.

   _____

**C** Look at the map in the reading passage and answer the questions.

INTERPRETING VISUAL INFORMATION

1. What does the map show?
   a. how many languages are disappearing
   b. the areas where languages are at risk of disappearing
   c. the places the Enduring Voices team is working

2. Which areas in the world have languages that are under severe threat?

   _____

   _____

3. Why do you think languages in these areas are facing the greatest threat? Discuss with a partner.

USING A T-CHART **B** Work with a partner. Think of both sides of the issue below. Write at least two pros and two cons. Then choose the side that you think is stronger.

| Issue: Everyone should start learning a second language at the age of three. | |
|---|---|
| **Pros** | **Cons** |
| • | • |
| • | • |

NOTICING **C** Read the sentence from a persuasive essay and answer the questions.

*Although it may be difficult for immigrant children to maintain both their native language and the dominant language of their new country, their parents should encourage them to be bilingual.*

1. What are the two sides of the argument the writer presents?

   Argument 1: _____

   Argument 2: _____

2. Which is the writer's main argument?

   _____

## LANGUAGE FOR WRITING Presenting Counterarguments

Arguments in a persuasive essay are more convincing and balanced when writers present and then refute the counterarguments—the arguments on the other side of the issue. Writers introduce counterarguments using **concession words and phrases** such as *while, even though,* and *although.*

COUNTERARGUMENT

***While** flying around the world to record speakers of disappearing languages may be expensive, protecting the valuable knowledge these languages contain is worth it.*

WRITER'S ARGUMENT

In addition, writers often use modals such as *may, might,* and *could* when presenting counterarguments to show that these arguments are weaker—less likely or certain—than their own arguments. Writers sometimes also present their own arguments with modals such as *must, have to,* and *should* to show that their arguments are stronger.

WEAKER

*While saving endangered languages **may** preserve some cultural or scientific information, we **must not** discourage children from learning the dominant language of their region.*

STRONGER

**D** Look back at the arguments in exercise C and answer the questions below.

1. Which word introduces the counterargument? _____

2. Which modal introduces the writer's main argument? _____

**E** Combine the sentences (1–3) using concession words. Add modals to the underlined verbs in the counterarguments.

*Example:* Argument: Not everyone can be effectively multilingual.

Counterargument: Being multilingual <u>is</u> an important skill today.

<u>Although being multilingual may be an important skill today, not everyone can be</u>
<u>effectively multilingual.</u>

1. Argument: Most children should learn Mandarin as a second language
   Counterargument: English <u>is</u> useful in some situations.

   _____

   _____

2. Argument: Mandarin is useful in the world of business.
   Counterargument: Mandarin <u>is</u> difficult to learn.

   _____

   _____

3. Argument: We must preserve smaller languages because of the important knowledge they contain.
   Counterargument: Language diversity <u>leads to</u> misunderstanding or conflict.

   _____

   _____

**F** Choose a point (pro or con) in exercise B and a related counterargument. Combine them into a sentence using concession words and modals.

_____

_____

_____

# REVISING PRACTICE

The draft below is a persuasive essay about whether companies should employ multilingual workers or train existing workers to be multilingual. Follow the steps to create a better second draft.

1. Add the sentences (a–c) in the most suitable spaces.
   a. Another reason is that language learning is far too time-consuming.
   b. If businesses hire people who are fluent in more than one language, they won't only save time and money, they will also have a diverse workforce with many points of view.
   c. While it may be possible to become fluent in a second language as an adult, experts believe that age greatly affects our language learning ability.

2. Now fix the following problems (d–f) in the essay.
   d. Add a modal to weaken a counterargument in paragraph B.
   e. Cross out a sentence that doesn't belong in paragraph B.
   f. Add a missing concession word in paragraph C.

**A**

Speaking a second language is an important skill in today's global economy. An employee who can do business in more than one language is a valuable asset to most companies. However, companies should hire employees who are already bi- or trilingual rather than train them. Corporations should not pay for their employees to learn a second language because some people may not have the ability to learn another language, and the process takes too much time.

**B**

One reason companies should not pay for their employees to learn a second language is that some people may not be capable of learning an extra language. _____ According to the Ets-Hokin Center for Language Acquisition, research shows that "people's ability to learn a foreign language deteriorates as they age." Studies also show that people have a harder time learning to play an instrument when they are older. In addition, memorization is an important part of language learning. Even though an employee performs their job well, it does not mean that they have a good enough memory to retain information needed to learn a second language.

**C**

_____ Some language programs promise fluency in a short period of time, the average language learner needs constant and long-term exposure to a second language in order to become even somewhat fluent. For example, according to the article "How Long Does It Take to Learn a New Language?," a typical employee taking two hours off work each day to study a language would take several years to become even relatively fluent. From a financial perspective, it is more cost-effective to have that employee do their job for those two hours a day.

**D**

The fact that language learning is time-consuming and that there is a risk that some learners will fail in their attempt indicate that it isn't a good idea for companies to invest in language training. Rather, it is more cost-effective to hire employees who are already bi- or trilingual. _____

# EDITING PRACTICE

**Read the information below.**

In sentences with concession words and modals, remember to use:

- a comma after the concession clause.
- a subject and a verb in both clauses.
- the base form of a verb after a modal.
- a weaker modal to present counterarguments, and stronger ones for the main arguments.

**Correct one mistake with concession words and modals in each sentence (1–3).**

1. While language instruction may being expensive, it is important that children learn a second language in order to compete in the global economy.

2. Even though Mandarin may soon become an important world language, probably will be challenging for learners to learn its writing system.

3. Although French was an important language in the past it shouldn't be an official UN language; there are just too few native speakers.

# UNIT REVIEW

**Answer the following questions.**

1. Do you think we should save dying languages? Why or why not?

   _____

   _____

   _____

2. What are some examples of concession words?

   _____

   _____

   _____

3. Do you remember the meanings of these words? Check (✓) the ones you know. Look back at the unit and review the ones you don't know.

   Reading 1:

   ☐ acquire **AWL**    ☐ anticipate **AWL**    ☐ competence

   ☐ considerably **AWL**    ☐ constitute **AWL**    ☐ expand **AWL**

   ☐ furthermore **AWL**    ☐ lead to    ☐ linguistic

   ☐ native

   Reading 2:

   ☐ combine    ☐ critically    ☐ die out

   ☐ express    ☐ highly    ☐ perspective **AWL**

   ☐ political    ☐ rapidly    ☐ rate

   ☐ roughly

# NOTES

# TRUTH AND DECEPTION 4

The Malaysian orchid mantis deceives its prey with its flower-like appearance.

**A** **Look at the information on these pages and answer the questions.**

1. What kinds of lies are most common?

2. Why did the people or organizations listed below lie? In which categories of the chart would you put the lies they told?

Nixon: _____ Barnum: _____
White Sox: _____

**B** **Match the words in blue to their definitions.**

_____ (v) to hide the truth about a mistake or wrongdoing

_____ (v) to give false information or guide someone wrongly

_____ (n) lack of guilt, the state of having done nothing wrong

In 2016, behavioral scientist Timothy Levine conducted a survey to find out why people lie. He asked approximately 500 participants from five countries—including Guatemala, Egypt, and the United States—to describe a time that they lied or that someone lied to them. He found that there were four main categories of reasons that people **mislead** others: to protect oneself; to promote oneself; to impact others—that is, to protect them or to harm them; and for reasons that are not clear.

The infographic breaks down the four ▶ main categories into more specific reasons for lying, such as to **cover up** a mistake (to protect oneself) and to gain financial benefits (to promote oneself).

# FAMOUS LIES

## Richard Nixon

TIM MCDONAGH

In June 1972, five men broke into the Watergate building in Washington, D. C. to photograph documents and secretly record phone conversations in order to help President Richard Nixon win his reelection campaign. Nixon denied all involvement and asserted his **innocence**, declaring, "I am not a crook." But the White House cover-up failed, and Nixon resigned from office.

## P. T. Barnum

TIM MCDONAGH

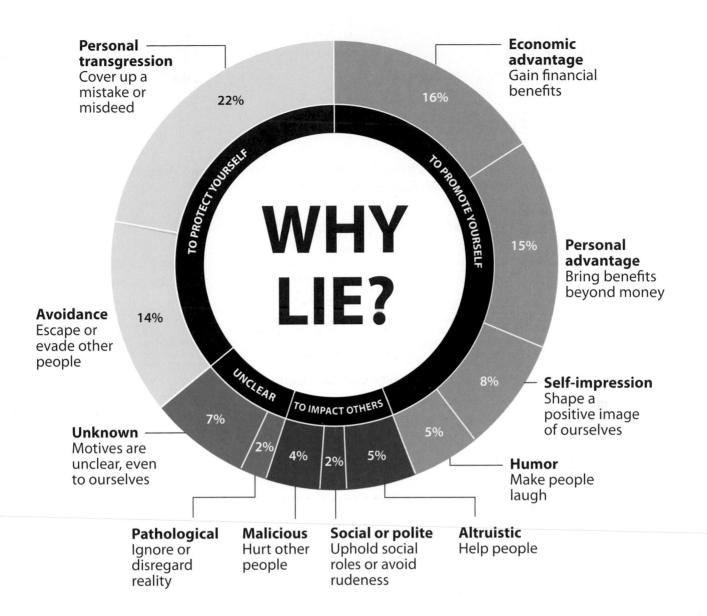

## WHY LIE?

**TO PROTECT YOURSELF**

**Personal transgression**
Cover up a mistake or misdeed — 22%

**Avoidance**
Escape or evade other people — 14%

**Unknown**
Motives are unclear, even to ourselves — 7%

**UNCLEAR**

**TO PROMOTE YOURSELF**

**Economic advantage**
Gain financial benefits — 16%

**Personal advantage**
Bring benefits beyond money — 15%

**Self-impression**
Shape a positive image of ourselves — 8%

**Humor**
Make people laugh — 5%

**TO IMPACT OTHERS**

**Pathological**
Ignore or disregard reality — 2%

**Malicious**
Hurt other people — 4%

**Social or polite**
Uphold social roles or avoid rudeness — 2%

**Altruistic**
Help people — 5%

P. T. Barnum, a showman and businessman from the United States, was famous for promoting and profiting from elaborate hoaxes. In 1835, for example, Barnum claimed that a woman in one of his shows was Joice Heth, George Washington's nursemaid, who would have been 161 years old. Crowds paid to see "the greatest natural and national curiosity in the world." After her death, however, an examination of the woman's body found her to be no more than 80 years old.

## The 1919 Chicago White Sox

TIM MCDONAGH

Nearly a century ago, some members of the Chicago White Sox baseball team accepted a huge amount of money to deliberately lose the 1919 World Series. The eight players who took the bribe were caught and banned from the game for life.

# Reading

## PREPARING TO READ

BUILDING
VOCABULARY

**A** The words in **blue** below are used in the reading passage. Read the sentences. Then match the correct form of each word to its definition.

> A polygraph, or lie detector, is a machine designed to **automatically** recognize when a person is lying.
>
> According to a study in *Nature Neuroscience*, a person's **capacity** for dishonesty increases each time they lie; that is, as they lie more, they get better at it.
>
> The **emergence** of new social science data in the form of studies and surveys continually improves our understanding of human behavior.
>
> The harmless appearance of a box jellyfish is incredibly **deceptive**—its venom is among the most deadly in the world.
>
> Kang Lee, a **prominent** behavioral psychologist, has done extensive research into the development of lying in children.
>
> Frank Abagnale, Jr., was able to fly around the world for free by impersonating an airline pilot. When he was found to be an **impostor**, he was jailed for six months.

1. _____ (adj) giving an appearance or impression that is misleading or untrue

2. _____ (adj) important and well-known

3. _____ (n) a person who dishonestly pretends to be someone else

4. _____ (n) the process of something coming into existence

5. _____ (n) the amount that something is able to produce

6. _____ (adv) done without thinking

BUILDING
VOCABULARY

**B** Complete the definitions with the words in the box. Use a dictionary to help you.

| deceitful | gullible | fundamental | prone to | systematically | thrive |
|---|---|---|---|---|---|

1. If someone is _____, they behave in a dishonest way.

2. To _____ is to become successful or to grow and increase in strength.

3. If a person is _____ doing something, they do it often and will likely do it again.

4. If someone is _____, they can be easily tricked.

5. If you do something _____, you do it following a fixed method or plan.

6. A _____ part of something is a basic and essential aspect of it.

**C** Note answers to the questions below. Then discuss with a partner.

1. Are people in certain professions more **prone to** lying than others? Why or why not?

_____

_____

2. How can you tell if someone is being **deceitful**?

_____

_____

3. Do you think we become less **gullible** as we get older? Explain your answer.

_____

_____

**D** Work with a partner. Make a list of things that people often lie about. Note your ideas below.

_____

_____

_____

**E** Skim the passage. How many of your ideas in **D** are mentioned?

**Leonardo DiCaprio (center) plays Frank Abagnale, Jr., in the 2002 movie *Catch Me If You Can*.**

# WHY WE LIE

by Yudhijit Bhattacharjee

> Honesty may be the best policy, but scheming and dishonesty may be part of what makes us human.

🎧 Track 5

**The history of humankind** is filled with skilled and practiced liars. Many are criminals who spin lies and weave **deceptive** tales to gain unjust rewards. Some are politicians who lie to gain power, or to cling to it. Sometimes people lie to boost their image, others lie to **cover up** bad behavior. Even the academic science community—a world largely devoted to the pursuit of truth—has been shown to contain a number of deceivers. But the lies of **impostors**, swindlers, and boasting politicians are just a sample of the untruths that have characterized human behavior for thousands of years.

A

Lying, it turns out, is something that most of us are very skilled at. We lie with ease, in ways big and small, to strangers, co-workers, friends, and loved ones. Our **capacity** for lying is as **fundamental** to us as our need to trust others. Being **deceitful** is part of our nature, so much so that we might say that to lie is human.

B

Our natural tendency to lie was first **systematically** documented by Bella DePaulo, a social psychologist at the University of California, Santa Barbara. Two decades ago, DePaulo and her colleagues asked 147 adults to note down every instance they lied or tried to **mislead** someone during one week. The researchers found that the subjects lied on average one or two times a day. Most of these untruths were harmless, intended to hide one's failings or to protect the feelings of others. Some lies were excuses—one person blamed their failure to take out the garbage on not knowing where it needed to go. Yet other

C

lies—such as a claim of being a diplomat's son—were told to present a false image. While these were minor transgressions, DePaulo and other colleagues observed [in a later study] that most people have, at some point, told one or more "serious lies": hiding an affair from a husband or wife, for example, or making false claims on a college application.

That human beings should universally possess a talent for deceiving one another shouldn't surprise us. Researchers speculate that lying as a behavior arose not long after the **emergence** of language. The ability to manipulate others without using physical force may have helped us compete for resources—something similar to the evolution of deceptive strategies like camouflage[1] in the animal kingdom. "Lying is so easy compared to other ways of gaining power," notes ethicist[2] Sissela Bok of Harvard University, one of the most **prominent** thinkers on the subject. "It's much easier to lie in order to get somebody's money or wealth than to hit them over the head or rob a bank."

D

As dishonesty has come to be recognized as a fundamental human trait, social science researchers and neuroscientists have sought to understand the nature and roots of the behavior. How and when do we learn to lie? What are the psychological foundations of dishonesty? And why do we believe lies so easily?

E

[1]**Camouflage** is the way in which some animals are colored and shaped so that they cannot easily be seen in their surroundings.
[2]An **ethicist** is someone who studies questions about what is morally right and wrong.

**Lying is something of a developmental milestone**—like learning to walk and talk. Parents often find their children's lies troubling, as they signal the beginning of a loss of **innocence**. However, Kang Lee, a psychologist at the University of Toronto, sees the emergence of the behavior in toddlers as a reassuring sign that their cognitive growth is on track.

To study lying in children, Lee and his colleagues use a simple experiment. They ask kids to guess the identity of hidden toys, based only on an audio clue. For the first few toys, the clue is obvious—a bark for a dog, a meow for a cat—and the children answer easily. Then they play a sound that has nothing to do with the toy. "So you play Beethoven, but the toy's a car," Lee explains. The experimenter leaves the room pretending to take a phone call—a lie for the sake of science—and asks the child not to peek[3] at the toy. Returning, the experimenter asks the child for the answer, then follows up with the question: "Did you peek?"

Using hidden cameras, Lee and his researchers have discovered that the majority of children can't resist[4] peeking. The percentage of children who peek and then lie about it depends on their age. Among two-year-olds who peek, only about one third lie about it. Among three-year-olds, half lie. And by age eight, approximately 80 percent of the children tested claim they didn't peek.

Kids also get better at lying as they get older. When asked to guess the identity of the toy (that they have secretly looked at), three- and four-year-olds typically give the right answer straightaway—they don't realize that this reveals that they cheated. At seven or eight, kids learn to deliberately give a wrong answer at first, or they try to make their answer seem like a reasoned guess.

Five- and six-year-old kids fall in between. In one study, Lee used a Barney the dinosaur toy. One five-year-old girl denied that she had looked at the toy, which was hidden under a cloth. Then she told Lee she wanted to feel it before guessing. "So she puts her hand underneath the cloth, closes her eyes, and says, 'Ah, I know it's Barney,'" Lee recalls. "I ask, 'Why?' She says, 'Because it feels purple.'"

What drives this increase in lying sophistication[5] is the development of a child's ability to put himself or herself in someone else's shoes. Known as "theory of mind," this is the facility we acquire for understanding the beliefs, intentions, and knowledge of others. Also fundamental to lying is the brain's executive function: the abilities required for planning, making decisions, and self-control. This explains why the two-year-olds who lied and lied well in Lee's experiments performed better on tests of theory of mind and executive function than those who didn't.

---

[3]If you **peek** at something, you have a quick look at it, often secretly.
[4]If you **resist** doing something, you stop yourself from doing it even though you would like to.

[5]If something has a high level of **sophistication**, it is more advanced or complex than others.

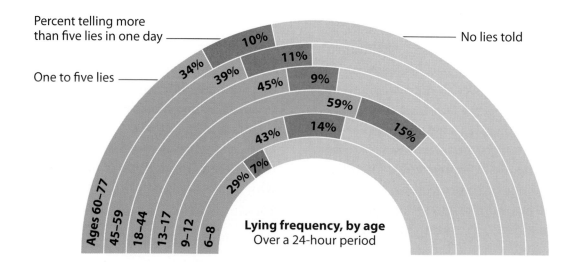

Percent telling more than five lies in one day ——— 10%

One to five lies ———

No lies told ———

**Lying frequency, by age**
Over a 24-hour period

Ages 60–77: 34% | 39% | 11%
45–59: 45% | 9%
18–44: 59% | 15%
13–17: 43% | 14%
9–12: 29% | 7%
6–8:

As we grow older, much of the knowledge we use to navigate the world comes from what others tell us. Without the implicit[6] trust that we place in human communication, we would be paralyzed[7] as individuals and cease to have social relationships. "We get so much from believing, and there's relatively little harm when we occasionally get duped," says Tim Levine, a psychologist at the University of Alabama.

Being programmed to trust makes us naturally **gullible**. "If you say to someone, 'I am a pilot,' they are not sitting there thinking: 'Maybe he's not a pilot. Why would he say he's a pilot?' They don't think that way," says Frank Abagnale, Jr. Now a security consultant, Abagnale's cons[8] as a young man—including forging checks and pretending to be an airline pilot—inspired the 2002 movie *Catch Me If You Can.* "This is why scams work," he says. "When the phone rings and the caller ID says it's the Internal Revenue Service,[9] people **automatically** believe it is the IRS. They don't realize that someone could manipulate the caller ID."

Robert Feldman, a psychologist at the University of Massachusetts, calls that "the liar's advantage." "People are not expecting lies, people are not searching for lies," he says, "and a lot of the time, people want to hear what they are hearing." We put up little resistance[10] to the deceptions that please or comfort us—such as false praise or the promise of impossibly high investment returns. And when we deal with people who have wealth, power, and status, the lies appear to be even easier to swallow.

Researchers are now learning that we are **prone to** believe some lies even when they're clearly contradicted by evidence. These insights suggest that our skill at deceiving others—combined with our vulnerability[11] to being deceived—is especially consequential in the age of social media. Research has shown, for example, that we are especially prone to accepting lies that affirm our worldview. False news stories **thrive** on the Internet and in social media because of this vulnerability, and disproving them does not tend to lessen their power. This is because people assess the evidence presented to them through a framework of preexisting beliefs and prejudices, says George Lakoff, a cognitive linguist at the University of California, Berkeley. "If a fact comes in that doesn't fit into your frame, you'll either not notice it, or ignore it, or ridicule it, or be puzzled by it—or attack it if it's threatening."

What then might be the best way to impede the rapid advance of untruths into our collective lives? The answer isn't clear. Technology has opened up a new frontier for deceit, adding a 21st-century twist to the age-old conflict between our lying and trusting selves.

[11]**Vulnerability** is the state of being open to attack or damage.

*Adapted from "Why We Lie," by Yudhijit Bhattacharjee, National Geographic Magazine June 2017.*

---

[6]If someone has **implicit** trust in something, they trust absolutely, without any doubts.

[7]If you are **paralyzed**, you are unable to act or function properly.

[8]Short for confidence trick, a **con** is a trick in which someone deceives you, usually with the intention of gaining money or power.

[9]In the United States, the **Internal Revenue Service (IRS)** is the government authority that collects taxes.

[10]To **put up resistance** to something means to refuse to accept it and try to prevent it.

**Yudhijit Bhattacharjee is an award-winning writer whose features and essays on science, espionage, cybercrime, and medicine have appeared in *The New Yorker, The New York Times Magazine, National Geographic, Wired,* and other magazines.**

# UNDERSTANDING THE READING

UNDERSTANDING
MAIN IDEAS

**A** Check (✓) the four topics that the writer covers in the reading passage.

a. ☐ the reasons that people lie

b. ☐ how often people lie

c. ☐ why people believe lies

d. ☐ cross-cultural differences in lying

e. ☐ the emotional effects of lying and being deceptive

f. ☐ the relationship between lying and cognitive development

IDENTIFYING
SUPPORTING IDEAS

**B** Complete the summaries below with details from the reading passage.

| We are natural liars | We are naturally gullible |
|---|---|
| Psychologist Bella DePaulo asked 147 adults to write down every time they attempted to ¹_____ for a period of ²_____. | Tim Levine says that getting tricked occasionally isn't a problem because we get so much benefit from believing others. |
| It was discovered that people lied an average of ³_____ times a day, though most of these lies were ⁴_____. | According to Frank Abagnale, Jr., scams work because we are trained to ⁸_____ people in authority. |
| In a later study, DePaulo and other colleagues learned that most people have told ⁵_____ lies at some point in their lives. | Psychologist Robert Feldman says that we don't ⁹_____ lies; we want to believe what we hear, especially if it's ¹⁰_____. |
| Researchers think that humans began lying with the invention of ⁶_____ because it's easier to lie to get what we want than it is to use ⁷_____. | Research shows we tend to believe things that are clearly ¹¹_____. Cognitive linguist George Lakoff explains that we are more likely to believe lies when they fit into our preexisting ¹²_____. |

IDENTIFYING
MEANING FROM
CONTEXT

**C** Find and underline the following words and phrases in the reading passage. Use the context to match each word or phrase to its definition.

| | | |
|---|---|---|
| **unjust** (paragraph A) | **manipulate** (paragraph D) | **reassuring** (paragraph F) |
| **on track** (paragraph F) | **get duped** (paragraph L) | **twist** (paragraph P) |

1. _____ (adj) not fair

2. _____ (adj) making you feel less worried about something

3. _____ (v) to control or influence a person or situation, often unfairly

4. _____ (n) an unexpected and significant occurrence

5. _____ (v) to be tricked into believing something that is not true

6. _____ (adj) following a course likely to result in success

> **CRITICAL THINKING** Writers sometimes refer to scientific research and behavioral studies to support their main ideas. When you read information about an experiment or study, it's important to ask yourself questions to **evaluate the research** and identify any limitations. For example, you can ask:
> - How did the researchers choose or gather the subjects?
> - Were the subjects representative of the population studied in terms of age, gender, and so forth?
> - Were the results reliable? Were they interpreted correctly?

**D** Work with a partner. Note answers to the questions below. Then discuss with a partner.

CRITICAL THINKING:<br>EVALUATING<br>RESEARCH

1. Do you think the people in DePaulo's study record their answers truthfully? Why or why not?

_____

_____

2. Which untruths do you think the participants were more likely to record?

_____

_____

3. Is there a better way to do the study? What might you have done differently?

_____

_____

**E** Look back at the quote from George Lakoff in the final sentence of paragraph O. What does he mean by "doesn't fit into your frame"? Discuss your ideas with a partner.

CRITICAL THINKING:<br>INTERPRETING

**F** Think of a news story that you heard about that turned out to be false. Note answers to the questions below. Then discuss with a partner.

CRITICAL THINKING<br>RELATING

1. What was the story about?

_____

_____

2. How could you tell the story was false?

_____

_____

3. What problems do you think misleading news stories like this could cause?

_____

_____

# DEVELOPING READING SKILLS

> ### READING SKILL  Understanding a Research Summary
>
> When writers refer to studies, they often summarize the main points of the research. These points usually include:
>
> - the **purpose** of the study (the question that they want to answer)
> - the **method** (how they set up and carried out the study)
> - the **results** (what the study found)
> - and the **conclusion** (the significance of the results—that is, how they answered the research question)
>
> When reading a research summary, it's useful to highlight these points and identify them in the margins.

UNDERSTANDING A
RESEARCH SUMMARY

**A** The sentences below summarize a piece of research known as "The Matrix Experiments." What does each sentence describe? Write **purpose**, **method**, **results**, or **conclusion**.

In the experiments, over 40,000 volunteers were given a five-minute test with 20 simple math problems. They were then asked to state how many questions they had answered correctly.  _____

The Matrix Experiments were a series of studies designed to measure dishonesty in adults.  _____

The results suggested that while lying is common, there are very few people who tell big lies.  _____

On average, 70% of people lied about their test results. But only 20 out of the 40,000 claimed to have solved all 20 problems.  _____

UNDERSTANDING A
RESEARCH SUMMARY

**B** Reread paragraphs G–I of the reading passage. Highlight and label the parts that explain the **purpose**, **method**, and **results** of Kang Lee's study.

UNDERSTANDING A
RESEARCH SUMMARY

**C** Write a concluding sentence to explain the significance of the results.

_____

_____

Video

# LEARNING TO LIE

In 2015, psychologist Kang Lee analyzed the lying habits of young children.

## BEFORE VIEWING

**A** In what situations might children tell lies? Discuss with a partner.

DISCUSSION

**B** Read about some more of psychologist Kang Lee's research. Then answer the questions.

LEARNING ABOUT THE TOPIC

What makes children good liars? For over 20 years, Kang Lee, a psychologist at the University of Toronto, has been studying how children lie. He has found that there are two key ingredients that make some children better liars than others. One is the ability to recognize that another person's knowledge of a situation may be less complete than your own. Known as "theory of mind," this ability allows a person to identify circumstances in which a lie might be believed. The second factor is self-control. In order to lie well, children have to be able to control their body language and their facial expressions. This is because, unless they are well controlled, a person's body and facial movements can often indicate that they are lying.

1. What are two skills children need in order to be good at telling lies?

   _____

   _____

2. Look back at the reading passage. Why does Kang Lee believe lying can be a good sign in children?

   _____

   _____

**C** The words in **bold** below are used in the video. Match the correct form of each word to its definition.

> In one of Lee's studies, a child peeked at a toy when he was told not to. Then he lied in order to cover up his **transgression**.
>
> We don't normally **condone** lying in children. In fact, many parents do not tolerate this behavior.
>
> Lee states that lying is a **milestone** in a child's life because when children start to do it, it's an indication that they are developing normally.

1. _____ (v) to approve of or allow something

2. _____ (n) the act of doing something wrong

3. _____ (n) an important stage in a process or journey

# WHILE VIEWING

**A** ▶ Watch the video. Circle the correct option to complete each sentence.

1. The purpose of the first experiment is to test a child's ability to **tell when someone is lying / tell white lies**.

2. The purpose of the second experiment is to test a child's ability to lie in order to **cover up a transgression / help another person**.

**B** ▶ Watch the video again. Complete the notes below.

| Experiment One—Method | Experiment Two—Method |
|---|---|
| • Researcher asks child series of questions | • Researcher plays card game with child |
| • Researcher gives child a prize | • Researcher tells child that if next answer is right, she will get a prize |

# AFTER VIEWING

**A** Kang Lee sees the ability to lie as a positive development in a child's life. How do you think a parent should react if their child lies to them? Discuss with a partner.

**B** Why does Kang Lee say that a world in which no one lies would be a very cruel place? Discuss with a partner.

# UNIT REVIEW

**Answer the following questions.**

1. What are two reasons people lie?

   _____

   _____

2. Why might someone believe a lie that is clearly contradicted by evidence?

   _____

   _____

3. Do you remember the meanings of these words? Check (✓) the ones you know. Look back at the unit and review the ones you don't know.

   ☐ automatically AWL     ☐ impostor AWL

   ☐ capacity AWL     ☐ innocence

   ☐ cover up     ☐ mislead

   ☐ deceitful     ☐ prominent

   ☐ deceptive     ☐ prone to

   ☐ emergence AWL     ☐ systematically

   ☐ fundamental AWL     ☐ thrive

   ☐ gullible

# VOCABULARY EXTENSION   UNIT 1

**WORD LINK**  *mis-*

The prefix *mis-* means "wrong or bad." For example, *mislead* means "to make someone think of something that is wrong or untrue."

Circle the correct words to complete the paragraph.

While most graphs accurately [1] **represent / misrepresent** data, some graphs can contain [2] **leading / misleading** information. One reason for this is that the designer of the graph simply made a [3] **calculation / miscalculation** with the numbers. Another reason is that the designer may have used an inappropriate scale. This can cause people to [4] **interpret / misinterpret** the significance of the information in the graph. A final reason is that the designer may have incorrectly compared two pieces of data. This is a [5] **use / misuse** of data because it shows a correlation that doesn't really exist.

# VOCABULARY EXTENSION   UNIT 3

**WORD PARTNERS**  adjective + *language*

Adding an adjective before the word *language* can provide more information about the kind of language you are talking about. Below are definitions of common collocations with *language*.

*native language*: the language you learn from birth

*body language*: communicating through gestures or facial expressions

*official language*: the language used legally in a country or organization

*foreign language*: a language used in a different country from your own

*technical language*: words and terms mainly understood in a particular professional field

Circle the correct word to complete each sentence.

1. The **native / body** language of Brazil is Portuguese.

2. Learning a **native / foreign** language when you are an adult can be much harder than when you are a child.

3. The two **official / technical** languages of the International Olympic Committee are English and French.

4. Sometimes you can tell how someone is feeling by looking at their **body / foreign** language.

5. Specialized fields, such as computer programming, often have their own **official / technical** language.

# VOCABULARY EXTENSION  UNIT 4

## WORD FORMS  Forming Nouns with -ance and -ence

The suffixes -ence and -ance indicate a noun form and are often made from adjectives ending in -ent or -ant (e.g., emergent—emergence). In addition, -ance can be added to some verbs to create nouns (e.g., appear—appearance).

**A**  Write the correct noun form using -ence or -ance. Check your answers in a dictionary.

1. independent          _____

2. intelligent          _____

3. dominant          _____

4. resist          _____

5. attend          _____

6. prominent          _____

## WORD FORMS  Word Forms of deceit

The word deceit can be formed into the following parts of speech:

**deceive** (v)          **deceit** (n)          **deceitful** (adj)          **deceitfully** (adv)

**B**  Complete each sentence with the correct form of deceit.

1. Frank Abagnale Jr.'s most elaborate_____ was probably his impersonation of an airline pilot.

2. By using a fake employee ID, he _____ an airline operator into thinking he was a pilot. He flew over one million miles.

3. Abagnale also became an attorney using a fake degree from Harvard Law School. One of his colleagues—a Harvard graduate—thought Abagnale was behaving _____ and started to investigate him.

4. Abagnale believes that he got away with these acts largely because people are generally very trusting and do not expect _____ behavior from others.

# Brief Writer's Handbook

## Understanding the Writing Process: The Seven Steps

### The Assignment

Imagine that you have been given the following assignment: *Write an essay in which you discuss one aspect of vegetarianism.* What should you do first? What should you do second, third, and so on? There are many ways to write, but most good writers follow certain steps in the writing process. These steps are guidelines that are not always followed in order.

Look at this list of steps. Which ones do you regularly do? Which ones have you never done?

STEP 1: Choose a topic.

STEP 2: Brainstorm.

STEP 3: Outline.

STEP 4: Write the first draft.

STEP 5: Get feedback from a peer.

STEP 6: Revise the first draft.

STEP 7: Proofread the final draft.

Next, you will see how one student, Hamda, went through the steps to do the assignment. First, read the final essay that Hamda gave her teacher.

### Essay 1

### Better Living as a Vegetarian

1       The hamburger has become a worldwide cultural icon. Eating meat, especially beef, is an integral part of many diverse cultures. Studies show, however, that the consumption of large quantities of meat is a major contributing factor toward a great many deaths, including the unnecessarily high number of deaths from heart-related problems. Although it has caught on slowly in Western society, vegetarianism is a way of life that can help improve not only the quality of people's lives but also their longevity.

2       Surprising as it may sound, vegetarianism can have beneficial effects on the environment. Because demand for meat animals is so high, cattle are being raised in areas where rain forests once stood. As rain forest land is cleared in order to make room for cattle ranches, the environmental balance is upset; this imbalance could have serious consequences for humans. The article "Deforestation: The hidden cause of global warming" by Daniel Howden explains that much of the current global warming is due to depletion of the rain forests.

3       More important at an individual level is the question of how eating meat affects a person's health. Meat, unlike vegetables, can contain very large amounts of fat. Eating this fat has been connected—in some research cases—to certain kinds of cancer. In fact, *The St. Petersburg*

*Times* reports, "There was a statistically significant risk for . . . gastric cancer associated with consumption of all meat, red meat and processed meat" (Rao, 2006). If people cut down on the amounts of meat they ate, they would automatically be lowering their risks of disease. Furthermore, eating animal fat can lead to obesity, and obesity can cause numerous health problems. For example, obesity can cause people to slow down and their heart to have to work harder. This results in high blood pressure. Meat is also high in cholesterol, and this only adds to health problems. With so much fat consumption worldwide, it is no wonder that heart disease is a leading killer.

4    If people followed vegetarian diets, they would not only be healthier but also live longer. Eating certain kinds of vegetables, such as broccoli, brussels sprouts, and cauliflower, has been shown to reduce the chance of contracting colon cancer later in life. Vegetables do not contain the "bad" fats that meat does. Vegetables do not contain cholesterol, either. Furthermore, native inhabitants of areas of the world where people eat more vegetables than meat, notably certain areas of Central Asia, routinely live to be over one hundred.

5    Some people argue that, human nature being what it is, it is unhealthy for humans to not eat meat. These same individuals say that humans are naturally carnivores and cannot help wanting to consume a juicy piece of red meat. However, anthropologists have shown that early humans ate meat only when other foods were not abundant. Man is inherently a herbivore, not a carnivore.

6    Numerous scientific studies have shown the benefits of vegetarianism for people in general. There is a common thread for those people who switch from eating meat to consuming only vegetable products. Although the change of diet is difficult at first, most never regret their decision to become a vegetarian. They feel better, and those around them comment that they look better than ever before. As more and more people are becoming aware of the risks associated with meat consumption, they too will make the change.

# Steps in the Writing Process

## Step 1: Choose a Topic

For this assignment, the topic was given: Write an essay on vegetarianism. As you consider the assignment topic, you have to think about what kind of essay you may want to write. Will you list different types of vegetarian diets? Will you talk about the history of vegetarianism? Will you argue that vegetarianism is or is not better than eating animal products?

Hamda chose to write an argumentative essay about vegetarianism to try to convince readers of its benefits. The instructor had explained that this essay was to be serious in nature and have facts to back up the claims made.

## Step 2: Brainstorm

The next step for Hamda was to brainstorm.

In this step, you write every idea about your topic that pops into your head. Some of these ideas will be good, and some will be bad; write them all. The main purpose of brainstorming is to write as many ideas as you can think of. If one idea looks especially good, you might circle that idea or put a check next to it. If you write an idea and you know right away that you are not going to use it, you can cross it out.

Brainstorming methods include making lists, clustering similar ideas, or diagramming your thoughts.

Look at Hamda's brainstorming diagram on the topic of vegetarianism.

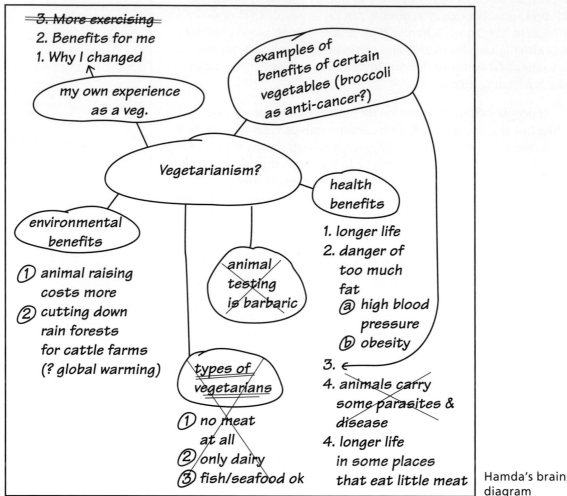

Hamda's brainstorming diagram

As you can see from the brainstorming diagram, Hamda considered many aspects of vegetarianism. Notice a few items in the diagram. As she organized her brainstorming, Hamda wrote "examples of benefits of certain vegetables" as a spoke on the wheel. Then she realized that this point would be a good number three in the list of health benefits, so she drew an arrow to show that she should move it there. Since one of Hamda's brainstorming ideas (types of vegetarians) seemed to lack supporting details and was not related to her other notes, she crossed it out.

## Getting the Information

How would you get the information for this brainstorming exercise?

- You might read a book or an article about vegetarianism.

- You could spend time searching online for articles on the subject.

- You could write a short questionnaire to give to classmates asking them about their personal knowledge of vegetarian practices.

- You could also interview an expert on the topic, such as a nutritionist.

> **Writer's Note**
>
> **Doing Research**
>
> To get a deeper understanding of your essay topic, you may choose to do some research. Remember that any information you get from an outside source needs to be credited in your essay. Writers do NOT use others' ideas in their writing without giving the proper credit.
>
> Take another look at Hamda's essay. Can you find the places where she used outside sources to back up her ideas?

## Step 3: Outline

Next, create an outline for the essay. Here is Hamda's rough outline that she wrote from her brainstorming notes.

I. Introduction
  A. Define vegetarianism
  B. List different types
  C. Thesis statement

II. Environmental benefits (Find sources to support!)
  A. Rain forests
  B. Global warming

III. Health issues (Find sources to support!)
  A. Too much fat from meat → obesity → diseases → cancer
  B. High blood pressure and heart disease
  C. Cancer-fighting properties of broccoli and cauliflower, etc.

IV. Counterargument and refutation
  A. Counterargument: Man is carnivore.
  B. Refutation

V. Conclusion
  A. Restate thesis
  B. Opinion: Life will improve.

## Supporting Details

After you have chosen the main points for your essay you will need to develop some supporting details. You should include examples, reasons, explanations, definitions, or personal experiences. In some cases, such as this argumentative essay on vegetarianism, it is a good idea to include outside sources or expert opinions that back up your claims.

One common technique for generating supporting details is to ask specific questions about the topic, for example:

What is it?

What happened?

How did this happen?

What is it like or not like? Why?

## Step 4: Write the First Draft

Next, Hamda wrote her first draft. As she wrote each paragraph of the essay, she paid careful attention to the language she used. She chose a formal sentence structure including a variety of sentence types. In addition, her sentences varied in length, with the average sentence containing almost 20 words. (Sentences in conversation tend to be very short; sentences in academic writing tend to be longer.) Hamda also took great care in choosing appropriate vocabulary. In addition to specific terminology, such as *obesity, blood pressure,* and *consumption,* she avoided the conversational *you* in the essay, instead referring to *people* and *individuals.*

In this step, you use information from your brainstorming session and outline to write the essay. This first draft may contain many errors, such as misspellings, incomplete ideas, and comma errors. At this point, you should not worry about correcting the errors. The main thing is to put your ideas into sentences.

You may feel that you do not know what you think about the topic yet. In this case, it may be difficult for you to write, but it is important to just write, no matter what comes out. Sometimes writing helps you think, and as soon as you form a new thought, you can write it.

# Better Living as a Vegetarian

*Wow — too abrupt? You don't talk about hamburgers anymore??*

(Do you like hamburgers?) Eating meat, especially beef, is an (interesting) part of the

*vocabulary?*

daily life around the world. In addition, this high (eating) of meat is a major contributing

*word choice?*

*causes*

*factor* ~~thing~~ that ~~makes~~ a great many deaths, including the unnecessarily high number of

deaths from heart-related problems. Vegetarianism has caught on slowly in some parts

*, and it*

of the world. (~~V~~egetarianism is a way of life that can help improve not only the quality of

*→ the quality but also the length*
*of people's lives*

people's lives but also people's longevity. ⟶

*This is not a topic sentence*

⎡ Because demand for meat animals is (so high., Cattle) are being raised in areas where

⎣ the rainforest once stood. As rain forest land is cleared in massive amounts in order to

make room for the cattle ranches, the environmental balance is being upset. This could

*For example,* *transition?*

have serious consequences for us in both the near and long term., How much of the current

global warming is due to man's disturbing the rain forest?

*You need a more specific topic relating to health.*

(Meat contains a high amount of fat.) Eating this fat has been connected in research

cases with certain kinds of cancer. Furthermore, eating animal fat can lead to obesity, and

obesity can cause many different kinds of diseases, for example, obesity can cause people

to slow down and their heart to have to word harder. This results in high blood pressure.

Meat is high in cholesterol, and this only adds to the health problems. With the high

consumption of animal fat by so many people, it is no wonder that heart disease is a

leading killer.

Hamda's first draft

On the other hand, eating a vegetarian diet can improve a person's health. And

*necessary?*

vegetables taste so good. In fact, it can even save someone's life. Eating certain kinds

of vegetables, such as broccoli, brussels sprouts, and cauliflower, has been shown to

reduce the chance of having colon cancer later in life. Vegetables do not contain

*combine sentences?*

the "bad" fats that meat does. Vegetables do not contain cholesterol, either. Native

inhabitants of areas of the world where mostly vegetables are consumed, notably

certain areas of the former Soviet republics, routinely live to be over one hundred.

*good sentence*

Although numerous scientific studies have shown the benefits of vegetarianism for people

in general, I know firsthand how my life has improved since I decided to give up meat entirely.

In 2006, I saw a TV program that discussed problems connected to animals that are raised for

food. The program showed how millions of chickens are raised in dirty, crowded conditions

*not related to your topic*

until they are killed. The program also talked about how diseases can be spread from cow or

pig to humans due to unsanitary conditions. Shortly after I saw this show, I decided to try life

without eating meat. Although it was difficult at first, I have never regretted my decision to

become a vegetarian. I feel better and my friends tell me that I look better than ever before.

Being a vegetarian has many benefits. Try it.

*This is too short! How about making a prediction or suggestion for the reader? The previous paragraph told how the writer became a vegetarian, so doesn't it make sense for the conclusion to say something like "I'm sure your life will be better too if you become a vegetarian"?*

*I like this essay. You really need to work on the conclusion.*

## Making Changes

As you write the first draft, you may want to add information or take some out. In some cases, your first draft may not follow your outline exactly. That is OK. Writers do not always stick with their original plan or follow the steps in the writing process in order. Sometimes they go back and forth between steps. The writing process is much more like a cycle than a line.

Reread Hamda's first draft with her teacher's comments.

## First Draft Tips

Here are some things to remember about the first draft copy:

- The first draft is not the final copy. Even native speakers who are good writers do not write an essay only one time. They rewrite as many times as necessary until the essay is the best that it can be.

- It is OK for you to make notes on your drafts; you can circle words, draw connecting lines, cross out words, or write new information. Make notes to yourself about what to change, what to add, or what to reconsider.

- If you cannot think of a word or an idea as you write, leave a blank space or circle. Then go back and fill in the space later. If you write a word that you know is not the right one, circle or underline it so you can fill in the right word later. Do not stop writing. When people read your draft, they can see these areas you are having trouble with and offer comments that may help.

- Do not be afraid to throw some sentences away if they do not sound right. Just as a good housekeeper throws away unnecessary things from the house, a good writer throws out unnecessary or wrong words or sentences.

The handwriting in the first draft is usually not neat. Sometimes it is so messy that only the writer can read it! Use a word-processing program, if possible, to make writing and revising easier.

## Step 5: Get Feedback from a Peer

Hamda used a peer editing sheet to get feedback on her essay draft. Peer editing is important in the writing process. You do not always see your own mistakes or places where information is missing because you are too close to the essay that you created. Ask someone to read your draft and give you feedback about your writing. Choose someone that you trust and feel comfortable with. While some people feel uneasy about peer editing, the result is almost always a better essay. Remember to be polite when you edit another student's paper.

## Step 6: Revise the First Draft

This step consists of three parts:

1. React to the comments on the peer editing sheet.
2. Reread the essay and make changes.
3. Rewrite the essay one more time.

## Step 7: Proofread the Final Draft

Most of the hard work is over now. In this step, the writer pretends to be a brand-new reader who has never seen the essay before. Proofread your essay for grammar, punctuation, and spelling errors and to see if the sentences flow smoothly.

Read Hamda's final paper again on pages 91–92.

Of course, the very last step is to turn the paper in to your teacher and hope that you get a good grade!

---

### Writer's Note

**Proofreading**

One good way to proofread your essay is to set it aside for several hours or a day or two. The next time you read your essay, your head will be clearer and you will be more likely to see any problems. In fact, you will read the composition as another person would.

# Editing Your Writing

While you must be comfortable writing quickly, you also need to be comfortable with improving your work. Writing an assignment is never a one-step process. For even the most gifted writers, it is often a multiple-step process. When you were completing your assignments in this book, you probably made some changes to your work to make it better. However, you may not have fixed all of the errors. The paper that you turned in to your teacher is called a first draft, which is sometimes referred to as a rough draft.

A first draft can often be improved. One way to improve an essay is to ask a classmate, friend, or teacher to read it and make suggestions. Your reader may discover that one of your paragraphs is missing a topic sentence, that you have made grammar mistakes, or that your essay needs better vocabulary choices. You may not always like or agree with the comments from a reader, but being open to changes will make you a better writer.

This section will help you become more familiar with how to identify and correct errors in your writing.

## Step 1

Below is a student's first draft for a timed writing. The writing prompt for this assignment was "For most people, quitting a job is a very difficult decision. Why do people quit their jobs?" As you read the first draft, look for areas that need improvement and write your comments. For example, does the writer use the correct verb tenses? Is the punctuation correct? Is the vocabulary suitable for the intended audience? Does the essay have an appropriate hook?

---

**There Are Many Reasons Why People Quit Their Jobs**

Joann quit her high-paying job last week. She had had enough of her coworkers' abuse. Every day they would make fun of her and talk about her behind her back. Joann's work environment was too stressful, so she quit. Many employees quit their jobs. In fact, there are numerous reasons for this phenomenon.

First, the job does not fit the worker. Job seekers may accept a job without considering their skills. Is especially true when the economy is slowing and jobs are hard to find. The workers may try their best to change themselves depending on the work. However, at some point they realize that they are not cut out in this line of work and end up quitting. This lack of understanding or ability make people feel uncomfortable in their jobs. So they begin to look for other work.

Another reason people quit their jobs is the money. Why do people work in the first place? They work in order to make money. If employees are underpaid, he cannot earn enough to support himself or his family. The notion of working, earning a decent salary, and enjoy life is no longer possible. In this case, low-paid workers have no choice but to quit their jobs and search for a better-paying position.

---

Perhaps the biggest situation that leads people to quit their jobs is personality conflicts. It is really difficult for an employee to wake up every morning, knowing that they will be spending the next eight or nine hours in a dysfunctional environment. The problem can be with bosses or coworkers but the result is the same. Imagine working for a discriminate boss or colleagues which spread rumors. The stress levels increases until that employee cannot stand the idea of going to work. The employee quits his or her job in the hope of finding a more calm atmosphere somewhere else.

Work should not be a form of punishment. For those people who have problems with not feeling comfortable on the job, not getting paid enough, and not respected, it *does* feel like punishment. As a result, they quit and continue their search for a job that will give them a sense of pride, safety, and friends.

# Step 2

Read the teacher's comments on the first draft of "There Are Many Reasons Why People Quit Their Jobs." Are these the same things that you noticed?

The title should NOT be a complete sentence.

### There Are Many Reasons Why People Quit Their Jobs

Consider changing your hook/introduction. The introduction here is already explaining one of the reasons for quitting a job. This information should be in the body of the essay. Suggestion: Use a "historical" hook describing how people were more connected to their jobs in the past than they are now.

Joann quit her high-paying job last week. She had had enough of her coworkers' abuse. Every

day they would make fun of her and talk about her behind her back. Joann's work environment

was too stressful, so she quit. Many employees quit their jobs. In fact, there are numerous reasons

for this phenomenon.

*Try to use another transition phrase instead of first, second, etc.*

add transition

(First,) the job does not fit the worker. ∧Job seekers may accept a job without considering their

*word choice—be more specific*     *fragment*

(skills.) <u>Is especially true when the economy is slowing and jobs are hard to find.</u> The workers may

*word choice—better: "adapt to"*

try their best to (change themselves depending on) the work. However, at some point they realize

*prep*

that they are not cut out (in) this line of work and end up quitting. This lack of understanding or

*S-V agreement*                                    *fragment*

ability (make) people feel uncomfortable in their (jobs. So) they begin to look for other work.

*word choice—be more specific*

Another reason people quit their jobs is the (money.) Why do people work in the first place?

They work in order to make money. If (employees) are underpaid, (he) cannot earn enough to

*pronoun agreement*

*// not parallel—use "-ing"*

support (himself) or (his family.) The notion of working, earning a decent salary, and (enjoy) life is

*word choice*     *Do you mean "underpaid"?*

no longer (possible.) In this case, (low-paid) workers have no choice but to quit their jobs and

search for a better-paying position.

*word choice—too vague*

Perhaps the (biggest) situation that leads people to quit their jobs is personality conflicts. It is

*word choice—avoid using "really"*     *pronoun agreement*

(really) difficult for an employee to wake up every morning, knowing that (they) will be spending

*add another descriptive word here*     *word choice—too vague*

the next eight or nine hours in a dysfunctional ∧ environment. The (problem) can be with bosses

*punc. (add comma)*     *word choice*

or coworkers but the result is the same. Imagine working for a (discriminate) boss or colleagues

*word form*     *S-V agreement*     *write it out—better: "can no longer"*

(which) spread rumors. The stress levels (increases) until that employee (can't) stand the idea of

*add transition*     *word choice—better: "serene"*

going to work. ∧ The employee quits his or her job in the hope of finding a more (calm) atmosphere

somewhere else.

*thought of as*     *word choice*

Work should not be ∧ a form of punishment. For those people who (have problems) with not

*// not parallel—use "-ing"*

feeling comfortable on the job, not getting paid enough, and (not respected,) it *does* feel like

punishment. As a result, they quit and continue their search for a job that will give them a

*word choice—better: "camaraderie"*

sense of pride, safety, and (friends.)

# Step 3

Now read the second draft of this essay. How is it the same as the first draft? How is it different? Did the writer fix all the sentence mistakes?

## Two Weeks' Notice

A generation ago, it was common for workers to stay at their place of employment for years and years. When it was time for these employees to retire, companies would offer a generous pension package and, sometimes, a token of appreciation, such as a watch, keychain, or other trinket. Oh, how times have changed. Nowadays, people—especially younger workers—jump from job to job like bees fly from flower to flower to pollinate. Some observers might say that today's workforce is not as serious as yesterday's. This is too simple an explanation, however. In today's society, fueled by globalization, recession, and other challenges, people quit their jobs for a number of valid reasons.

One reason for quitting a job is that the job does not fit the worker. In other words, job seekers may accept a job without considering their aptitude for it. This is especially true when the economy is slowing and jobs are hard to find. The workers may try their best to adapt themselves to the work. However, at some point they realize that they are not cut out for this line of work and end up quitting. This lack of understanding or ability makes people feel uncomfortable in their jobs, so they begin to look for other work.

Another reason people quit their jobs is the salary. Why do people work in the first place? They work in order to make money. If employees are underpaid, they cannot earn enough to support themselves or their families. The notion of working, earning a decent salary, and enjoying life is no longer viable. In this case, underpaid workers have no choice but to quit their jobs and search for a better-paying position.

Perhaps the most discouraging situation that leads people to quit their jobs is personality conflicts. It is extremely difficult for an employee to wake up every morning knowing that he or she will be spending the next eight or nine hours in a dysfunctional and often destructive environment. The discord can be with bosses or coworkers, but the result is the same. Imagine working for a bigoted boss or colleagues who spread rumors. The stress levels increase until that employee can no longer stand the idea of going to work. In the end, the employee quits his or her job with the hope of finding a more serene atmosphere somewhere else.

Work should not be thought of as a form of punishment. For those people who struggle with not feeling comfortable on the job, not getting paid enough, and not being respected, it *does* feel like punishment. As a result, they quit and continue their search for a job that will give them a sense of pride, safety, and camaraderie.

# Sentence Types

English sentence structure includes three basic types of sentences: simple, compound, and complex. These labels indicate how the information in a sentence is organized, not how difficult the content is.

## Simple Sentences

1. Simple sentences usually contain one subject and one verb.

   <u>S</u>  <u>V</u>
   [Kids] love television.

   <u>V</u>  <u>S</u>  <u>V</u>
   Does [this] sound like a normal routine?

2. Sometimes simple sentences can contain more than one subject or verb.

   <u>S</u>  <u>V</u>
   [Brazil and the United States] are large countries.

   <u>S</u>  <u>V</u>  <u>V</u>
   [Brazil] lies in South America and has a large population.

   <u>S</u>  <u>V</u>  <u>V</u>
   [We] traveled throughout Brazil and ended our trip in Argentina.

## Compound Sentences

Compound sentences are usually made up of two simple sentences (independent clauses). Compound sentences need a coordinating conjunction (connector) to combine the two sentences. The coordinating conjunctions include:

    for    and    nor    but    or    yet    so

Many writers remember these conjunctions with the acronym *FANBOYS*. Each letter represents one conjunction: F = *for*, A = *and*, N = *nor*, B = *but*, O = *or*, Y = *yet*, and S = *so*.

Remember that a comma is always used before a coordinating conjunction that separates the two independent clauses.

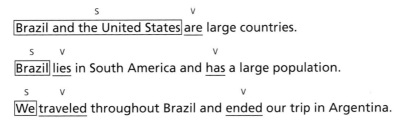

**for**  [Meagan] studied hard, **for** [she] wanted to pass the test.

**and**  [Meagan] studied hard, **and** [her classmates] studied, too.

**nor**  [Meagan] did not study hard, **nor** did [she] pass the test.

**but**  [Meagan] studied hard, **but** [her brother] did not study at all.

**or**  [Meagan] studied hard, **or** [she] would have failed the test.

**yet**  [Meagan] studied hard, **yet** [she] was not happy with her grade.

**so**  [Meagan] studied hard, **so** [the test] was easy for her.

Study the following examples of compound sentences. Draw a box around each subject, underline each verb, and circle each coordinating conjunction.

1. Brazil was colonized by Europeans, and its culture has been greatly influenced by this fact.

2. This was my first visit to the international section of the airport, and nothing was familiar.

3. Many people today are overweight, and being overweight has been connected to some kinds of cancer.

4. Barriers fell, markets opened, and people rejoiced in the streets because they anticipated a new life full of opportunities and freedom to make their own choices.

5. Should public school students make their own individual decisions about clothing, or should all students wear uniforms?

6. This question has been asked many times, but people are not in agreement about the ultimate punishment.

# Complex Sentences

Like compound sentences, complex sentences are made up of two parts. Complex sentences, however, contain one independent clause and, at least, one dependent clause. In most complex sentences, the dependent clause is an adverb clause.

# Complex Sentences (with Adverb Clauses)

Adverb clauses begin with subordinating conjunctions, which include the following:

while    although    after    because    if    before

Study the examples below. The adverb clauses are underlined, and the subordinating conjunctions are boldfaced.

The hurricane struck **while** we were at the mall.

**After** the president gave his speech, he answered most of the reporters' questions.

Unlike coordinating conjunctions, which join two independent clauses but are not part of either clause, subordinating conjunctions are actually part of the dependent clause.

| Joe played tennis | **after** Vicky watched TV. |
|---|---|
| independent clause | dependent clause |

The subordinating conjunction *after* does not connect the clauses *Joe played tennis* and *Vicky watched TV*; *after* is grammatically part of *Vicky watched TV*.

Remember that dependent clauses must be attached to an independent clause. They cannot stand alone as a sentence. If they are not attached to another sentence, they are called fragments, or incomplete sentences. Fragments are incomplete ideas, and they cause confusion for the reader. In a complex sentence, both clauses are needed to make a complete idea so the reader can understand what you mean. Look at these examples:

| Fragment: | After Vicky watched TV |
|---|---|
| Complete Sentence: | Joe played tennis after Vicky watched TV. |
| | or |
| Complete Sentence: | After Vicky watched TV, she went to bed. |

Study the following examples of complex sentences from the essays in this book. Draw a box around each subject, underline each verb, and circle each subordinating conjunction.

1. While the Northeast is experiencing snowstorms, cities like Miami, Florida, can have temperatures over 80 degrees Fahrenheit.

2. Although Brazil and the United States are unique countries, there are remarkable similarities in their size, ethnic diversity, and personal values.

3. Another bus arrived at the terminal, and the passengers stepped off carrying all sorts of luggage.

4. While it is true that everyone makes a blunder from time to time, some people do not have the courage to admit their errors because they fear blame.

5. Because almost every area has a community college, students who opt to go to a community college first can continue to be near their families for two more years.

# Additional Grammar Activities

The three example essays in this section feature different grammatical errors. Each paragraph highlights one kind of error. In each case, read the entire essay before you complete the activities.

Before you complete Activities 1–5, read the whole essay first. Then go back and complete each activity.

## ACTIVITY 1  Verb Forms

Read the paragraph and decide whether the five underlined verbs are correct. If not, draw a line through the verb and write the correct form above the verb.

**Essay 2**

### A Simple Recipe

1    "When in Rome, do as the Romans do" may sound ridiculous, but this proverb offer an important suggestion. If you travel to other countries, especially to a country that is very different from your own, you should keeping this saying in mind. For example, Japan has unique customs that is not found in any other country. If you traveled to Japan, you should find out about Japanese customs, taboos, and people beforehand.

## ACTIVITY 2  Verb Forms

Read this paragraph carefully. Then write the correct form of the verbs in parentheses.

2    One custom is that you should (take) _____ off your shoes before (enter) _____ someone's house. In Japan, the floor must always be kept clean because usually people (sit) _____, eat a meal, or even (sleep) _____ on the floor. Another custom

is giving gifts. The Japanese often (give) _____ a small gift to people who have (do) _____ favors for them. Usually this token of gratitude (give) _____ in July and December to keep harmonious relations with the receiver. When you (give) _____ someone such a gift, you should make some form of apology about it. For example, many Japanese will say, "This is just a small gift that I have for you." In addition, it is not polite to open a gift immediately. The receiver usually (wait) _____ until the giver has left so the giver will not be embarrassed if the gift (turn) _____ out to be defective or displeasing.

### ACTIVITY 3   Connectors

Read the paragraph carefully. Then fill in the blanks with one of these connectors:

because     in addition     even if     for example     first     but

3      _____, it is important to know about Japanese taboos. All cultures have certain actions that are considered socially unacceptable. _____ something is acceptable in one culture, it can easily be taboo in another culture. _____, chopsticks are used in many cultures, _____ there are two taboos about chopsticks etiquette in Japan. _____, you should never stand the chopsticks upright in your bowl of rice. _____ standing chopsticks upright is done at a funeral ceremony, this action is associated with death. Second, you must never pass food from one pair of chopsticks to another. Again, this is related to burial rites in Japan.

### ACTIVITY 4   Articles

There are 14 blanks in this paragraph. Read the paragraph and write the articles *a, an,* or *the* to complete the sentences. Some blanks do not require articles.

4      Third, it is important to know that Japanese people have _____ different cultural values. One of _____ important differences in _____ cultural values is _____ Japanese desire to maintain _____ harmony at all costs. People try to avoid causing any kind of dispute. If there is _____ problem, both sides are expected to compromise in order to avoid an argument. People are expected to restrain their emotions and put _____ goal of compromise above their individual wishes. Related to this is _____ concept of patience. Japanese put _____ great deal of

_____ value on _____ patience. Patience
also contributes to maintaining _____ good relations with
_____ everyone and avoiding _____ disputes.

## ACTIVITY 5  Prepositions

Read this paragraph and write the correct preposition in each blank. Choose from these prepositions: *into, in, to, about, with, of,* and *around.* You may use them more than once.

5        _____ conclusion, if you want to get along well
_____ the Japanese and avoid uncomfortable situations
when you go _____ Japan, it is important to take
_____ account the features _____ Japanese
culture that have been discussed here. Although it may be hard to
understand Japanese customs because they are different, knowing
_____ them can help you adjust to life in Japan. If you face
an unfamiliar or difficult situation when you are _____
Japan, you should do what the people _____ you do. In other
words, "When _____ Japan, do as the Japanese do."

> Before you complete Activities 6–12, read the whole essay. Then go back and complete each activity.

## ACTIVITY 6  Verb Forms

Read this paragraph carefully. Then write the correct form of the verbs in parentheses.

**Essay 3**

### Dangers of Corporal Punishment

1        What should parents do when their five-year-old child says
a bad word even though the child knows it is wrong? What should a
teacher (do) _____ when a student in the second grade
(call) _____ the teacher a name? When my parents (be)
_____ children forty or fifty years ago, the answer to these
questions was quite clear. The adult would spank the child immediately.
Corporal punishment (be) _____ quite common then. When
I was a child, I (be) _____ in a class in which the teacher got
angry at a boy who kept (talk) _____ after she told him to
be quiet. The teacher then (shout) _____ at the boy and, in

front of all of us, (slap) _____ his face. My classmates and
I were shocked. Even after twenty years, I still remember that incident
quite clearly. If the teacher's purpose (be) _____ to (teach)
_____ us to (be) _____ quiet, she did not
(succeed) _____. However, if her purpose was to create an
oppressive mood in the class, she succeeded. Because corporal punishment
(be) _____ an ineffective and cruel method of discipline, it
should never be (use) _____ under any circumstances.

**ACTIVITY 7** **Prepositions**

Read this paragraph carefully. Write the correct preposition in each blank. Use these prepositions: *in,*
*of,* and *for.*

2        Supporters _____ corporal punishment claim that
physical discipline is necessary _____ developing a child's
sense _____ personal responsibility. Justice Lewis Powell, a
former U.S. Supreme Court justice, has even said that paddling children
who misbehave has been an acceptable method _____
promoting good behavior and responsibility _____ school
children for a long time. Some people worry that stopping corporal
punishment in schools could result _____ a decline
_____ school achievement. However, just because a student
stops misbehaving does not mean that he or she suddenly has a better
sense _____ personal responsibility or correct behavior.

**ACTIVITY 8** **Articles**

Read the paragraph and write the articles *a, an,* or *the* to complete the sentences. Some blanks do not
require articles.

3        Corporal punishment is _____ ineffective way
to punish _____ child because it may stop a behavior
for a while, but it will not necessarily have _____
long-term effect. Thus, if an adult inflicts _____ mild
form of _____ corporal punishment that hurts the child
very little or not at all, it will not get rid of the bad behavior. Moreover,
because corporal punishment works only temporarily, it will have
to be repeated whenever the child misbehaves. It may then become
_____ standard response to any misbehavior. This can lead
to _____ frequent and more severe spanking, which may
result in _____ abuse.

**ACTIVITY 9** Comma Splices

Read this paragraph carefully and find the two comma splices. Correct them in one of two ways:
(1) change the comma to a period and make two sentences or (2) add a connector after the comma.

4       A negative effect of corporal punishment in school is that it makes some students feel aggressive toward parents, teachers, and fellow students. In my opinion, children regard corporal punishment as a form of teacher aggression that makes them feel helpless. Therefore, students may get frustrated if corporal punishment is used frequently. Furthermore, it increases disruptive behavior that can become more aggressive, this leads to school violence and bullying of fellow students. Supporters of corporal punishment believe that it is necessary to maintain a good learning environment, it is unfortunate that the opposite result often happens. The learning environment actually becomes less effective when there is aggressive behavior.

**ACTIVITY 10** Verb Forms

Read the paragraph and decide whether the underlined verbs are correct. If not, draw a line through the verb and write the correct form above it.

5       Last, corporal punishment may <u>result</u> in antisocial behavior later in life because it teaches children that adults <u>condone</u> violence as a solution to problems. Children who are <u>spank</u> learn that it is acceptable for a stronger person <u>using</u> violence against a weaker person. The concept of "might makes right" is <u>forced</u> upon them at a very early age. Furthermore, this concept teaches a lesson not only to those who are spanked but also to those who <u>witness</u> it. Studies of prisoners and delinquents <u>shows</u> that nearly 100 percent of the violent inmates at San Quentin and 64 percent of juvenile delinquents <u>was</u> victims of seriously abusive punishment during childhood. If serious punishment <u>causes</u> antisocial behavior, perhaps even milder punishment also <u>contribute</u> to violence. Research at the University of New Hampshire <u>will find</u> that children who were spanked between the ages of three and five <u>showed</u> higher levels of antisocial behavior when they <u>were observed</u> just two and four years later. This behavior included higher levels of beating family members, hitting fellow students, and defying parents. It is ironic that the behaviors for which teachers <u>punishing</u> students often get worse as a result of the spanking.

## ACTIVITY 11 Editing for Errors

There are seven errors in this paragraph. They are in word forms (two), articles (one), sentence fragments (one), verb tense (one), and subject-verb agreement (two). Mark these errors and write corrections.

6        For punishment to be effective, it must produce a great behavioral change, result in behavior that is permanent, and produce minimal side effects. However, none of these changes is a result of corporal punishment. Therefore, we should consider alternatives to corporal punishment. Because discipline is necessary to educate children. One of the alternatives are to emphasize students' positive behaviors. Some research shows that reward, praise, and self-esteem is the most powerful motivators for the learning. Other alternatives are to hold conferences with students to help them plan acceptable behave or to use school staff, such as psychologists and counselors. It is important to build better interpersonal relations between teachers and students. In addition to these alternatives, instruction that reaches all students, such as detention, in-school suspension, and Saturday school, is available to discipline and punishment unruly students, too. Alternatives to corporal punishment taught children to be self-disciplined rather than to be cooperative only because of fear.

## ACTIVITY 12 Editing for Errors

There are seven errors in this paragraph. They are in word forms (one), articles (three), sentence fragments (one), comma splices (one), and subject-verb agreement (one). Mark these errors and write the corrections.

7        In the conclusion, teachers should not use corporal punishment because it is ineffective in disciplining students and may have long-term negative effects on students. Moreover, teachers should not forget that love and understanding must be part of any kind of discipline. Discipline and love is not opposites, punishment must involve letting the children know that what they do is wrong and why punishment is necessary. Teachers should not just beat student with the hopeful that he will understand. It is important to maintain discipline without inflicting physical pain on students. Therefore, teachers should use effective and more humane alternatives. In order to bring about permanent behavioral changes.

Before you complete Activities 13–18, read the whole essay. Then go back and complete each activity.

Read the paragraph and write the articles *a, an,* or *the* to complete the sentences. Some blanks do not require articles.

## Washington and Lincoln

1        Perhaps no other names from _____ American history
are better known than the names of George Washington and Abraham
Lincoln. Both of these presidents made valuable contributions
to _____ United States during their presidency. In fact,
one could argue that _____ America would not be
_____ same country that it is today if either of these two
leaders had not been involved in _____ American politics.
However, it is interesting to note that although both leaders made
_____ significant contributions to _____
country, they lived in _____ quite different times and served
in _____ very different ways.

**ACTIVITY 14** **Verb Forms**

Read this paragraph carefully. Then write the correct form of the verbs in parentheses.

2        Everyone (know) _____ that George Washington
was the first president of the United States. What most people do not
(appreciate) _____ (be) _____ that Washington
(be) _____ a clever military leader. He served the country
in the early days of the Revolution by (help) _____ to
change the colonial volunteers from ragged farmers into effective soldiers.
Without Washington's bravery and military strategy, it is doubtful that
the colonies could have (beat) _____ the British. Thus,
without Washington, the colonies might never even have (become)
_____ the United States of America.

## ACTIVITY 15  Prepositions

Read this paragraph and write the correct preposition in each blank. Choose from these prepositions: *from, in, to, with, for, between,* and *of.* You may use them more than once.

3       Abraham Lincoln was the sixteenth president _____ the United States. He was elected president _____ 1860 during a controversial and heated period of American history. As more states applied _____ membership in the growing country, the issue _____ slavery kept surfacing. There was an unstable balance _____ slave states and free states. Each time another state was added _____ the Union, the balance of power shifted. Lincoln was _____ a free state, and many _____ the slave state leaders viewed Lincoln as an enemy of their cause _____ expand slavery. _____ the end, no compromise could be reached, and the slave states seceded _____ the United States in order to form their own independent country. Hostilities grew, and _____ 1861 the Civil War, or the War _____ the States as it is sometimes called, broke out. During the next four years, the Civil War ravaged the country. By the end of the war in 1865, the American countryside was _____ shambles, but the Union was once again intact. Through his military and political decisions, Lincoln is credited _____ saving the country _____ self-destruction.

## ACTIVITY 16  Editing for Errors

There are eight errors in this paragraph. They are in word forms (one), articles (two), modals (one), verb tense (two), and subject-verb agreement (two). Mark these errors and write corrections.

4       Washington and Lincoln was similarly in several ways. Both men are U.S. presidents. Both men served the United States during extremely difficult times. For Washington, the question is whether the United States would be able to maintain its independence from Britain. The United States was certainly very fragile nation at that time. For Lincoln, the question were really not so different. Would the United States to be able to survive during what was one of darkest periods of American history?

## ACTIVITY 17  Sentence Fragments

After you read this paragraph, find the three sentence fragments. Correct the fragments by (1) changing the punctuation and creating one complete sentence or (2) adding new words to make the fragment a complete sentence.

5   There were also several differences between Washington and Lincoln. Washington came from a wealthy aristocratic background. He had several years of schooling. Lincoln came from a poor background, and he had very little schooling. Another difference between the two involved their military roles. Washington was a general. He was a military leader. Became president. Lincoln never served in the military. He was a lawyer who early on became a politician. When he became president, he took on the role of commander in chief, as all U.S. presidents do. Despite his lack of military background or training. Lincoln made several strategic decisions that enabled the U.S. military leaders to win the Civil War. Finally, Washington served for two terms and therefore had eight years to accomplish his policies. Lincoln, on the other hand, was assassinated. While in office and was not able to finish some of the things that he wanted for the country.

## ACTIVITY 18  Editing for Errors

There are seven errors in this paragraph. They are in articles (two), verb tense (one), inappropriate words (one), word forms (one), number (singular and plural) (one), and subject-verb agreement (one). Mark these errors and make corrections.

6   The names George Washington and Abraham Lincoln is known even to people who have never been to the United States. Both of these patriots gave large part of their lives to help America make what it is today though they served the country in very different ways in complete different time in the American history. Although they were gone, their legacies and contributions continue to have an impact on our lives.

# Connectors

Using connectors will help your ideas flow. Remember that when connectors occur at the beginning of a sentence, they are often followed by a comma.

| Purpose | Coordinating Conjunctions (connect independent clauses) | Subordinating Conjunctions (begin dependent clauses) | Transitions (usually precede independent clauses) |
|---|---|---|---|
| Examples | | | For example, To illustrate, Specifically, In particular, |
| Information | and | | In addition, Moreover, Furthermore, |
| Comparison | | | Similarly, Likewise, In the same way, |
| Contrast | but | while, although | In contrast, However, On the other hand, Conversely, Instead, |
| Refutation | | | On the contrary, |
| Concession | yet | although though even though it may appear that | Nevertheless, Even so, Admittedly, Despite this, |
| Emphasis | | | In fact, Actually, |
| Clarification | | | In other words, In simpler words, More simply, |
| Reason/Cause | for | because since | |
| Result | so | so so that | As a result, As a consequence, Consequently, Therefore, Thus, |
| Time Relationships | | after as soon as before when while until whenever as | Afterward, First, Second, Next, Then Finally, Subsequently, Meanwhile, In the meantime, |
| Condition | | if even if unless provided that when | |

## Telling a Story/Narrating

| Words and Phrases | Examples |
|---|---|
| When I was NOUN / ADJ, I would VERB. | When I was a child, I would go fishing every weekend. |
| I had never felt so ADJ in my life. | I had never felt so anxious in my life. |
| I never would have thought that… | I never would have thought that I could win the competition. |
| Then the most amazing thing happened. | I thought my bag was gone forever. Then the most amazing thing happened. |
| Whenever I think back to that time, … | Whenever I think back to my childhood, I am moved by my grandparents' love for me. |
| I will never forget NOUN | I will never forget my wedding day. |
| I can still remember NOUN / I will always remember NOUN | I can still remember the day I started my first job. |
| NOUN was the best / worst day of my life. | The day I caught that fish was the best day of my life. |
| Every time S + V, S + V. | Every time I used that computer, I had a problem. |
| This was my first NOUN | This was my first time traveling alone. |

## Showing Cause and Effect

| Words and Phrases | Examples |
|---|---|
| Because S + V / Because of S + V | Because of the traffic problems, it is easy to see why the city is building a new tunnel. |
| NOUN can trigger NOUN<br>NOUN can cause NOUN | An earthquake can trigger tidal waves and can cause massive destruction. |
| Due to NOUN | Due to the economic sanctions, the unemployment rate skyrocketed. |
| On account of NOUN / As a result of NOUN / Because of NOUN | On account of the economic sanctions, the unemployment rate skyrocketed. |
| Therefore, NOUN / As a result, NOUN / For this reason, NOUN / Consequently, NOUN | Markets fell. Therefore, millions of people lost their life savings. |
| NOUN will bring about NOUN | The use of the Internet will bring about a change in education. |
| NOUN has had a positive / negative effect on NOUN | Computer technology has had both positive and negative effects on society. |
| The correlation… is clear / evident. | The correlation between junk food and obesity is clear. |

## Stating an Opinion

| Words and Phrases | Examples |
|---|---|
| Without a doubt, doing NOUN is ADJECTIVE idea / method / decision / way. | Without a doubt, walking to work each day is an excellent way to lose weight. |
| Personally, I believe / think / feel / agree / disagree / suppose that NOUN | Personally, I believe that using electronic devices on a plane should be allowed. |
| Doing NOUN should not be allowed. | Texting in class should not be allowed. |
| In my opinion / view / experience, NOUN | In my opinion, talking on a cell phone in a movie theater is extremely rude. |
| For this reason, NOUN / That is why I think NOUN | For this reason, voters should not pass this law. |

| | |
|---|---|
| There are many benefits / advantages to NOUN. | There are many benefits to swimming every day. |
| There are many drawbacks / disadvantages to NOUN. | There are many drawbacks to eating meals at a restaurant. |
| I am convinced that S + V. | I am convinced that nuclear energy is safe and energy efficient. |
| NOUN should be required / mandatory. | Art education should be required of all high school students. |
| I prefer NOUN to NOUN. | I prefer rugby to football. |
| To me, banning / prohibiting NOUN makes sense. | To me, banning cell phones while driving makes perfect sense. |
| For all of these important reasons, S + V. | For all of these important reasons, cell phones in schools should be banned. |
| Based on NOUN, S + V. | Based on the facts presented, high-fat foods should be banned from the cafeteria. |

## Arguing and Persuading

| Words and Phrases | Examples |
|---|---|
| It is important to remember S + V | It is important to remember that school uniforms would only be worn during school hours. |
| According to a recent survey, S + V | According to a recent survey, 85 percent of high school students felt they had too much homework. |
| Even more important, S + V | Even more important, statistics show the positive effects that school uniforms have on behavior. |
| Despite this, S + V | Despite this, many people remain opposed to school uniforms. |
| S must / should / ought to | Researchers must stop unethical animal testing. |
| For these reasons, S + V | For these reasons, public schools should require uniforms. |
| Obviously, S + V | Obviously, citizens will get used to this new law. |
| Without a doubt, S + V | Without a doubt, students ought to learn a foreign language. |
| I agree that S + V; however, S + V | I agree that a college degree is important; however, getting a practical technical license can also be very useful. |

## Giving a Counterargument

| Words and Phrases | Examples |
|---|---|
| Proponents / Opponents may say S + V | Opponents of uniforms may say that students who wear uniforms cannot express their individuality. |
| On the surface this might seem logical / smart / correct; however, S + V | On the surface this might seem logical; however, it is not an affordable solution. |
| S + V; however, this is not the case. | The students could attend classes in the evening; however, this is not the case. |
| One could argue that S + V, but S + V | One could argue that working for a small company is very exciting, but it can also be more stressful than a job in a large company. |
| It would be wrong to say that S + V | It would be wrong to say that nuclear energy is 100 percent safe. |
| Some people believe that S + V | Some people believe that nuclear energy is the way of the future. |

| | |
|---|---|
| *Upon further investigation*, S + V | *Upon further investigation*, one begins to see problems with this line of thinking. |
| *However, I cannot agree with this idea.* | Some people think logging should be banned. *However, I cannot agree with this idea.* |
| *Some people may say* (one opinion), *but I* (opposite opinion.) | *Some people may say that* working from home is lonely, *but I* believe that working from home is easy, productive, and rewarding. |
| *While* NOUN *has its merits*, NOUN… | *While* working outside the home *has its merits*, working from home has many more benefits. |
| *Although it is true that…*, S + V | *Although it is true that* taking online classes can be convenient, it is difficult for many students to stay on task. |

## Reacting/Responding

| Words and Phrases | Examples |
|---|---|
| TITLE *by* AUTHOR *is a / an* … | *Harry Potter and the Goblet of Fire* by J.K. Rowling *is an* entertaining book to read. |
| *My first reaction to the prompt / news / article was / is* NOUN | *My first reaction to the article was* fear. |
| *When I read / look at / think about* NOUN, *I was amazed / shocked / surprised* … | *When I read* the article, *I was surprised* to learn of his athletic ability. |

# NOTES

# NOTES

# NOTES